SECOND EDITION

Worksheets
Don't Grow Dendrites

SECOND EDITION

Worksheets
Don't Grow Dendrites

20
Instructional
Strategies
That Engage
the Brain

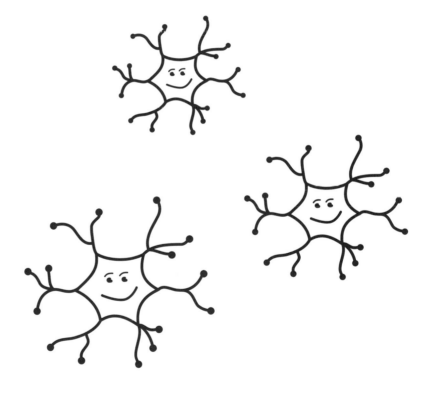

Marcia L. Tate

CORWIN
A SAGE Company

For information:

Corwin
A SAGE Company
2455 Teller Road
Thousand Oaks, California 91320
www.corwin.com

SAGE Pvt. Ltd.
B 1/I 1 Mohan Cooperative
    Industrial Area
Mathura Road, New Delhi 110 044
India

SAGE Ltd.
1 Oliver's Yard
55 City Road
London, EC1Y 1SP
United Kingdom

SAGE Asia-Pacific Pte. Ltd.
33 Pekin Street #02-01
Far East Square
Singapore 048763

Printed in the United States of America

Library of Congress Cataloging-in-Publication Data

Tate, Marcia L.
Worksheets don't grow dendrites : 20 instructional strategies that engage the brain/Marcia L. Tate.—2nd ed.
    p. cm.
Includes bibliographical references and index.
ISBN 978-1-4129-7850-7 (pbk.)
    1. Effective teaching—Handbooks, manuals, etc. 2. Lesson planning—Handbooks, manuals, etc. 3. Learning. I. Title.

LB1025.3.T29 2010
371.3028—dc22   2009051869

This book is printed on acid-free paper.

10   11   12   13   14   10   9   8   7   6   5   4   3   2   1

Acquisitions Editor:	Carol Chambers Collins
Associate Editor:	Megan Bedell
Editorial Assistant:	Allison Scott and Sarah Bartlett
Production Editor:	Veronica Stapleton
Copy Editor:	Codi Bowman
Typesetter:	C&M Digitals (P) Ltd.
Proofreader:	Charlotte Waisner
Indexer:	Sheila Bodell
Cover Designer:	Rose Storey

Contents

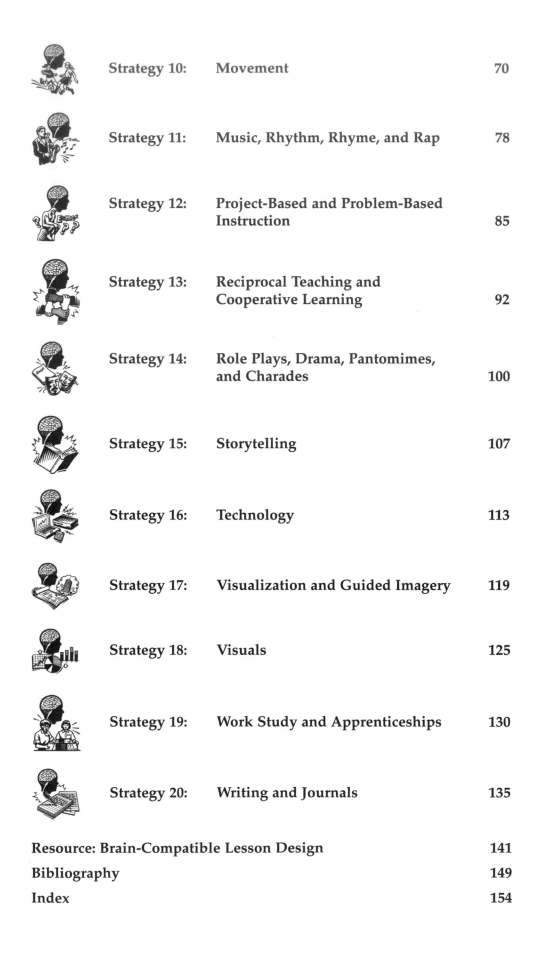

Introduction

20 Instructional Strategies That Engage the Brain

SCENARIO I ■

Let me tell you a true story. Visualize the following classrooms, if you will.

Mrs. Taylor teaches civics at Mainstreet Middle School. Lecture is her primary method of delivering instruction. Sometimes, the lectures last more than half the period. Today, the objective is to teach the branches of the federal government, and as usual, she is delivering a 30-minute talk on the three branches. She has no accompanying visuals and is depending on students to retain her content simply from listening to her talk and taking notes. Some of the higher-achieving students are paying close attention because they know that much of the information will appear on the midterm exam. Other students are maintaining eye contact with Mrs. Taylor while thinking about everything except the branches of the government. Several students are engaged in conversation and are promptly reprimanded. Mrs. Taylor doesn't even realize that most of the class stopped listening to her lectures during the first few days and weeks of school.

During the second half of the period, Mrs. Taylor changes her strategy so she can more actively engage students. She decides to have students round-robin orally read the chapter in the textbook. She assigns sections of the chapter in the order in which students are seated with the expectation that they will take turns reading their assigned sections aloud. What she hasn't noticed is that when the first student is reading aloud, all other students who have assignments are counting down to their section and prereading so they will not sound *stupid* when it is time for them to read aloud. Because the brain can only pay conscious attention to one thing at a time, this means that these students are not paying a bit of attention to the person who is reading. However, neither is the remainder of the class. Because some students are better oral readers than others, many students are finding this activity boring and much of the attention of the class is diverted. Some are talking, others are doodling, and others have their heads on their desks while still others are staring into space. After about a 20-minute period, students are told to use the remainder of the class time to answer the questions at the end of the chapter in writing and to complete for homework any questions not finished during the period. The bell rings and students run over one another as they race for the door.

SCENARIO II ■

Mr. Stewart teaches the same course at Midway Middle School. His students absolutely love him because they never quite know what to expect from day-to-day in his class. He has very few, if any, behavior problems. Mr. Stewart must cover the same curriculum as Mrs. Taylor; however, the two classrooms bear little resemblance to one another. Mr. Stewart is also teaching the branches of the federal government, but he is introducing the three branches while drawing a graphic organizer on the board as a visual. Students are asked to draw the visual in their notes so they will have a mind map to help them remember what is being taught. The graphic organizer consists of the three branches, a box underneath each that tells what each branch does, and a listing of which government positions are included in which branch. As Mr. Stewart completes the first branch, *judicial,* he stops and has students reteach what was just taught to their partners. Then he proceeds to the *executive* branch, continually asking, both students who volunteer and those who do not volunteer, questions to check for understanding.

As he finishes the third branch, *legislative,* Mr. Stewart engages students in a role play that is both memorable and lots of fun. He has made three signs, one for each branch of the government, and he places those signs in three different corners of the room. Then, Mr. Stewart moves around the room with his *magic wand* (a wand that lights up at the end and makes a noise), anointing students with the power of a government official. For example, one student is *anointed* as a Supreme Court Justice, another is anointed as the secretary of state, another is a senator, another serves in the house of representatives, and yet another is the vice president. Every student in class is assigned a role and asked to get up and go stand in the corner that represents the branch in which they belong. Once all students commit to a branch by moving to the appropriate corner, Mr. Stewart goes to each corner of the room and, one by one, asks students what positions they represent. The class determines whether the student is standing in the correct branch. With the exception of two, every student has selected the correct branch and the class celebrates their success with a loud, original cheer. Mr. Stewart summarizes the lesson by tossing a ball randomly to students and asking them questions about the lesson. The bell rings and Mr. Stewart stands at his door bidding a fond farewell to each student until tomorrow.

BRAIN-COMPATIBLE INSTRUCTION ■

Two middle school classes are both teaching the same content but using very different methodology. Which teacher would you rather have? Better yet, which teacher would you rather be? When you consider which teacher stands the best chance of getting the concept into the long-term memory of students' brains, no doubt, you would consider the latter class. Why?

One learns to do by doing.

—Aristotle

Tell me, I forget.

Show me, I remember.

Involve me, I understand!

—Old Chinese Proverb

Thousands of years of history support one major concept. When students are actively engaged in experiences with content, they stand a much better chance of learning and remembering what we want them to know. Yet with increased emphasis on *high-stakes testing,* teachers are apt to spend the majority of time using worksheets and lecture to teach lower-level concepts that can be best assessed by paper and pencil.

Learning-style theorists (Gardner, 1983; Marzano, 2007; McCarthy, 1990; and Sternberg & Grigorenko, 2000) and educational consultants (Jensen, 2008; Jensen, 2009b; Sousa, 2006; and Wolfe, 2001) have concluded that there are some instructional strategies that, by their very nature, result in long-term retention. Those strategies are addressed in numerous books about the brain but are not delineated in any one text. For the past 14 years, I have been studying the awesome functions of brain cells. Through my extensive reading, participation in workshops and courses with experts on the topic, and my observations of best practices in classrooms throughout the world, I have synthesized these instructional strategies into 20 methods for delivering instruction. And they work for the three following reasons:

1. They increase academic achievement for *all* of the following students: students who are in gifted classes, regular education classes, and special education classes; students who are in elementary, middle, and high school; students for whom English is a second language; and students who are learning across the curriculum.

2. They decrease behavior problems by minimizing the boredom factor in class and increasing the confidence factor in those students who would use their inadequacy as a cause for misbehavior.

3. They make teaching and learning fun for all grade levels so even students taking calculus are just as excited about learning as the kindergarten student is on the first day of school.

The 20 strategies are as follows:

1. Brainstorming and discussion
2. Drawing and artwork
3. Field trips
4. Games
5. Graphic organizers, semantic maps, and word webs
6. Humor
7. Manipulatives, experiments, labs, and models
8. Metaphors, analogies, and similes
9. Mnemonic devices
10. Movement

11. Music, rhythm, rhyme, and rap

12. Project-based and problem-based instruction

13. Reciprocal teaching and cooperative learning

14. Role plays, drama, pantomimes, and charades

15. Storytelling

16. Technology

17. Visualization and guided imagery

18. Visuals

19. Work-study and apprenticeships

20. Writing

President George Herbert Walker Bush declared the 1990s as the *decade of the brain.* Today, cofounder of Microsoft Paul Allen and others are investing millions into the continued study of the miracle of the brain. Teachers should be the first to avail themselves of this information because they are teaching the brains of students each and every day. In fact, I tell teachers that the next time they complete a résumé, they need to include that they are not only *teachers but also gardeners,* better known as *dendrite growers* because every time students learn something new in their classrooms, they grow a new brain cell, called a dendrite.

Refer to Figure 0.1 on page 8 for a correlation of these 20 strategies to Howard Gardner's Theory of Multiple Intelligences as well as to the four major modalities—(1) visual, (2) auditory, (3) kinesthetic, and (4) tactile. Each lesson that incorporates multiple modalities not only increases students' test scores but also stands a better chance of being remembered by students long after the teacher-made, criterion-referenced, or standardized tests are over. After all, isn't that what matters—long-term retention?

The book you are about to read attempts to accomplish four major objectives:

1. Review the research regarding the 20 brain-compatible strategies, as well as best practices in instruction regardless of the content area

2. Supply more than 200 examples of the application of the 20 strategies in teaching objectives at a variety of grade levels and in multiple content areas

3. Provide time and space at the end of each chapter for the reader to reflect on the application of the strategies as they apply directly to the reader's specific objectives

4. Demonstrate how to plan and deliver unforgettable lessons by asking the five questions on the lesson plan format contained in the Resource section of the book

The brain-compatible activities in each chapter are only samples of lessons that can be produced when the strategies are incorporated from kindergarten to calculus. They are intended only to get the reader's brain cells going, as they think up a multitude of additional ways to deliver brain-compatible instruction to their students.

When you really examine the list of 20, you will find that they are used most frequently in the lower elementary grades. When the strategies begin to disappear from the repertoire of teachers is about the same time that students' academic achievement, confidence, and love for school also diminish. The challenge is becoming so severe that when I pick up the *TIME* magazine dated April 17, 2006 (Thornburgh, 2006), the cover story is titled "Dropout Nation." It appears that the United States is not graduating approximately 30% of its high school students according to the article. In many major inner cities, the number can be as high as 50% to 60%. If a business were losing 30% to 60% of its clients per year, how long would it remain in business? The answer, of course, is *not very long.*

There are various reasons for the aforementioned dilemma, and no one person has all the answers. However, part of the answer lies in the following sign I saw posted on the wall in a teachers' lounge: *If students do not learn the way we teach them, then we must teach them the way they learn.* There are 20 ways to teach and 20 ways to learn.

This book is the foundational text in a series of multiple books about *growing dendrites.* The books are as follows:

- *Worksheets Don't Grow Dendrites: 20 Instructional Strategies That Engage the Brain*
- *Sit & Get Won't Grow Dendrites: 20 Professional Learning Strategies That Engage the Adult Brain*
- *Reading and Language Arts Worksheets Don't Grow Dendrites: 20 Literacy Strategies That Engage the Brain*
- *Shouting Won't Grow Dendrites: 20 Techniques for Managing a Brain-Compatible Classroom*
- *Mathematics Worksheets Don't Grow Dendrites: 20 Numeracy Strategies That Engage the Brain PreK–8.*

The activities outlined in each chapter of this text are designed to be starting points for planning lessons that are intended to be brain-compatible and are in no way meant to be an exhaustive list of possibilities. The advantage of having activities that range from kindergarten through Grade 12 in the same book is that the reader can easily select activities that will meet the needs of students performing below, on, and above grade level and can, therefore, more easily differentiate instruction. You will also find that an activity designated for a specific grade range can be taken as is or easily adapted to fit the grade level that the reader is teaching. Therefore, as you peruse this text, examine not only those activities in each content area that are age or grade appropriate but also look for ones at other grade levels that can easily meet your needs once you change the conceptual level of the material.

The reflection page at the end of each chapter enables readers to apply the activities read to their students or to enter activities that they have created. The lesson planning section helps the reader synthesize the process of planning unforgettable lessons by asking five pertinent questions.

Turn the page and begin your journey down a path that may help to revolutionize your instructional practices or support the effectiveness of some of the practices that you are currently using. At any rate, in many classrooms the fun has gone out of teaching and learning. Put it back while simultaneously growing their dendrites!

Comparison of Brain-Compatible Instructional Strategies to Learning Theory		
Brain-Compatible Strategies	Multiple Intelligences	Visual, Auditory, Kinesthetic, Tactile (VAKT)
Brainstorming and discussion	Verbal-linguistic	Auditory
Drawing and artwork	Spatial	Kinesthetic/tactile
Field trips	Naturalist	Kinesthetic/tactile
Games	Interpersonal	Kinesthetic/tactile
Graphic organizers, semantic maps, and word webs	Logical-mathematical/spatial	Visual/tactile
Humor	Verbal-linguistic	Auditory
Manipulatives, experiments, labs, and models	Logical-mathematical	Tactile
Metaphors, analogies, and similes	Spatial	Visual/auditory
Mnemonic devices	Musical-rhythmic	Visual/auditory
Movement	Bodily-kinesthetic	Kinesthetic
Music, rhythm, rhyme, and rap	Musical-rhythmic	Auditory
Project-based and problem-based learning	Logical-mathematical	Visual/tactile
Reciprocal teaching and cooperative learning	Verbal-linguistic	Auditory
Role plays, drama, pantomimes, charades	Bodily-kinesthetic	Kinesthetic
Storytelling	Verbal-linguistic	Auditory
Technology	Spatial	Visual/tactile
Visualization and guided imagery	Spatial	Visual
Visuals	Spatial	Visual
Work study and apprenticeships	Interpersonal	Kinesthetic
Writing and journals	Intrapersonal	Visual/tactile

Figure 0.1

Acknowledgments

It is my belief that every student comes to school with an inherent gift, a package, so to speak. It is the educator's job to unwrap this gift by finding the most viable means through which each student can excel. As society has changed, so has the packaging, necessitating the need for alternative ways of unwrapping these packages.

My gratitude goes to those educational consultants who are giving us additional ways to unwrap these gifts by translating the findings of the neuroscientists into educational practice and to those teachers who use interactive strategies daily to engage the brains of their students.

Speaking of gifts, I am deeply grateful for family members and professional educators who have supported me and assisted me with the writing of my books. To my husband and best friend, Tyrone, whose steadfast belief and constant encouragement enable me to unwrap each day with enthusiasm and a belief that all things are possible.

To my dearest children—Jennifer, Jessica, and Christopher, I write this book for them as much as anyone because their learning styles are as different as their personalities. Teachers could unwrap Jenny's gifts by involving her in hands-on activities. Jessie could always adapt her gifts to the instruction provided. Chris, on the other hand, needed to be bodily engaged in the task at hand. He had to draw, build, and move to be successful. Unless his teachers used these strategies, school was a struggle for my son. I dedicate this book to them and to the numerous parents in my workshops who have told me that their children are similar to mine.

To the associates who present for our company, Developing Minds, Inc., thank you for using your gifts to help me spread the word. To our administrative assistants, Carol and Sadira, your gifts of organization and technical expertise enable me to enhance my gifts. Working with you to improve instruction for all students is truly a present.

About the Author

Marcia L. Tate is the former executive director of professional development for the DeKalb County Schools in Decatur, Georgia. During her 30-year career with the district, she has been a classroom teacher, reading specialist, language arts coordinator, and staff development executive director. Marcia was named Staff Developer of the Year for the state of Georgia, and her department was selected to receive the Exemplary Program award for the state.

Marcia is currently an educational consultant and has presented her workshops to audiences all over the United States and the world, including Australia, Canada, Egypt, New Zealand, and Singapore. She is the author of the following five bestsellers: *Worksheets Don't Grow Dendrites: 20 Instructional Strategies That Engage the Brain*; *Sit & Get Won't Grow Dendrites: 20 Professional Learning Strategies That Engage the Adult Brain*; *Reading and Language Arts Worksheets Don't Grow Dendrites: 20 Literacy Strategies That Engage the Brain*; *Mathematics Worksheets Don't Grow Dendrites: 20 Numeracy Strategies That Engage the Brain*; and *Shouting Won't Grow Dendrites: 20 Techniques for Managing a Brain-Compatible Classroom*. She has also written a number of published articles and chapters that have been included in other books. Participants in her workshops call them some of the best ones they have ever attended because Marcia models the 20 strategies in her books to actively engage her audiences.

Dr. Tate received her bachelor's degree in psychology and elementary education from Spelman College in Atlanta, her master's in remedial reading from the University of Michigan in Ann Arbor, and her specialist and doctorate degrees in educational leadership from Georgia State University and Clark Atlanta University respectively.

Marcia is married to Tyrone Tate and is the proud mother of three children, Jennifer, Jessica, and Christopher. If she had known how wonderful it would be to be a grandmother, Marcia would have had her two grandchildren, Aidan and Christian, before she had her children. With her husband, she owns the company Developing Minds, Inc. and can be contacted by calling her company at (770) 918-5039, by e-mailing her at marciata@bell south.net, or by visiting her Web site at www.developingmindsinc.com.

Strategy 1

Brainstorming and Discussion

WHAT: DEFINING THE STRATEGY

In my book *Shouting Won't Grow Dendrites*, I created the following rhyme:

> *They can't talk in class.*
>
> *They can't talk in the hall.*
>
> *They can't talk in the cafeteria.*
>
> *They can't talk at all!*

Yet teachers are talking with one another every chance they get—in the lounge, in the cafeteria, in faculty meetings. . . . Need I continue? Are teachers expecting behaviors of students that are unnatural to the brain and those that they themselves would fail to follow?

When people open their mouths to speak, they send more oxygen to the brain. Oxygen is essential to healthy brain development. If the brain is deprived of oxygen for three to six minutes, it is declared dead. I have been in some classrooms where students were breathing, but it was hard to tell. The teacher was doing all the talking while students had their heads on desks, were staring out of the window, or were daydreaming. Students who have opportunities to brainstorm a variety of ideas with their peers without the fear of criticism or sarcasm are those who naturally improve their comprehension and higher-order thinking skills. Consider the following cross-curricular discussion starters:

- The answer is 156. What is the question?
- Discuss the design of an experiment that tests your hypothesis.
- Let's brainstorm other endings to our story.
- If you had been Anne Frank in *The Diary of Anne Frank,* how would you have dealt with her dilemma?

WHY: THEORETICAL FRAMEWORK

When students talk about a topic, they will understand it better because their brains not only mentally process the information but also verbally process it. (Allen, 2008)

Brainstorming or group discussion activities, in cooperation with graphic organizers, encourage all students to contribute. (Jensen, 2007)

Adolescents need to debate issues or participate in discussions around topics relevant to them. This should occur in a physically and psychologically safe environment. (Caine, Caine, McClintic, & Klimek, 2005)

Students up to the age of 10 learn better when an academic discussion is directed by the teacher. Adolescents and adults benefit from discussions led by a cooperative group. (Jensen, 2007)

The most widely known technique for simulating creativity in the brain is probably the act of brainstorming where all ideas are accepted and there is a greater chance of reaching a workable solution. (Gregory & Parry, 2006)

Students with special needs benefit when the class works in groups of fewer than six and the teacher uses directed response questioning so that students have a chance to think aloud. (Jensen, 2007)

Teachers can guide students through very difficult solutions to mathematics problems by using a series of well-thought-out questions that address process rather than procedure. (Posamentier & Jaye, 2006)

Discussion and questioning during whole class or cooperative group learning enable the brain to clarify concepts and hook new information with the information that the brain already knows. (Brooks & Brooks, 1993)

HOW: INSTRUCTIONAL ACTIVITIES

WHO: Elementary/Middle/High
WHEN: Before the lesson
CONTENT AREA(S):   All

• Prior to the reading of a story or unit of study, have students peruse any pictures, captions, bold headings, charts, graphs, and so forth to determine what the story or unit will be about. Have them brainstorm a list of questions to be answered as the unit or story is being read. The questions will give students a purpose for reading.

WHO: Elementary/Middle/High
WHEN: During a lesson
CONTENT AREA(S):   All

- Give students a content-area question to which there is more than one appropriate answer. Students brainstorm as many ideas as possible in a designated time while complying with the following DOVE guidelines:
  - **Defer judgment**
  - **One idea at a time**
  - **Variety of ideas**
  - **Energy on task**

WHO:	Elementary/Middle/High
WHEN:	During a lesson
CONTENT AREA(S):	All

- Have students work with peers in *families* of four to six. During the lesson, stop periodically and have families discuss answers to questions related to what is being taught. For example, in math class, students could compare their answers to the homework assignment, and when answers differ, they could engage in a discussion to reach consensus as to the correct answer. Have students stay together with their families long enough to build relationships and then change the composition of the families.

WHO:	Elementary/Middle/High
WHEN:	During or after a lesson
CONTENT AREA(S):	All

- When asking questions in class or creating teacher-made tests, provide opportunities for all students to be successful by asking both knowledge or short-answer questions as well as those that enable students to use their reasoning, critical-thinking, and creative-thinking skills. Refer to "Bloom's Taxonomy Revised" (Figure 1.1, page 15) to ensure that students have opportunities to answer questions at all levels of the revised taxonomy, particularly those above the *knowledge* level.

WHO:	Elementary/Middle/High
WHEN:	During or after the lesson
CONTENT AREA(S):	All

- During cooperative group discussions or as students create original questions for content-area assessments following a unit of study, have them use the question stems in Figure 1.1. These stems will help to ensure that questions are created that represent all levels of the revised Bloom's taxonomy.

WHO:	Elementary/Middle/High
WHEN:	During the lesson
CONTENT AREA(S):	All

- During discussions, sentence starters similar to the ones listed here are particularly effective for English language learners because they enable all students to take an active part:

o I realize that . . .
o I agree with _____ that _____.
o I would like to add to _____'s idea.
o I don't understand what _____ meant when she said _____.
(Coggins, Kravin, Coates, & Carrol, 2007)

WHO: Elementary/Middle/High
WHEN: During the lesson
CONTENT AREA(S): All

- Use the **think, pair, share** technique with students. Pose a question or discussion topic to the class. Have them *think* of an individual answer. Then have them *pair* with a peer and *share* their answer. Then call on both volunteers and nonvolunteers to respond to the entire class.

WHO: Elementary/Middle/High
WHEN: During a lesson
CONTENT AREA(S): All

- When asking a discussion question, wait a minimum of five to seven seconds to allow students' brains opportunities to reason out the answer. If, after a five-second minimum, the student does not respond, either rephrase the question, provide additional information, give a clue, or provide the student with question structures or frames such as the following:

    o Why is ____ different from ____?
    o How is this answer similar to the previous answer?
    o What is another way to say it?

WHO: Elementary/Middle/High
WHEN: During a lesson
CONTENT AREA(S): All

- Present a controversial issue to the class, such as, "How can we reduce the high school dropout rate in the United States?" Divide the class in half and have them research and prepare a debate for one side of the issue or another. Then, actually, role-play the debate by having students take turns serving on opposing teams and orally presenting their arguments to the class. You can be the judge on which side was more convincing at the culmination of the debate.

Bloom's Taxonomy Revised

Bloom's Taxonomy (1956) has stood the test of time. Recently, Anderson & Krathwohl (2001) have proposed some minor changes to include the renaming and reordering of the taxonomy. This reference reflects those recommended changes.

I. REMEMBER (KNOWLEDGE)
(shallow processing: drawing out factual answers, testing recall, and recognition)

Verbs for Objectives	Model Questions	Instructional Strategies
Choose	Who?	Highlighting
Describe?	Where?	Rehearsal
Define?	Which one?	Memorizing
Identify	What?	Mnemonics
Label	How?	
List	What is the best one?	
Locate	Why?	
Match	How much?	
Memorize	When?	
Name	What does it mean?	
Omit		
Recite		
Recognize		
Select		
State		

(Continued)

Figure 1.1 (Continued)

II. UNDERSTAND (COMPREHENSION)
(translating, interpreting, and extrapolating)

Verbs for Objectives	Model Questions	Instructional Strategies
Classify	State in your own words.	Key examples
Defend	What does this mean?	Emphasize connections
Demonstrate	Give an example.	Elaborate concepts
Distinguish	Condense this paragraph.	Summarize
Explain	State in one word . . .	Paraphrase
Express	What part doesn't fit?	STUDENTS explain
Extend	What exceptions are there?	STUDENTS state the rule
Give Example	What are they saying?	"Why does this example . . . ?"
Illustrate	What seems to be . . . ?	create visual representation
Indicate	Which are facts?	(concept maps, outlines, flow
Interrelate	Is this the same as . . . ?	charts organizers, analogies, pro/con grids) PRO/CON
Interpret	Read the graph (table).	Note: The faculty member can show them, but *they* have to do it.
Infer	Select the best definition.	Metaphors, rubrics, heuristics
Judge	What would happen if . . . ?	
Match	Explain what is happening.	
Paraphrase	Explain what is meant.	
Represent	What seems likely?	
Restate	This represents . . .	
Rewrite	Is it valid that . . . ?	
Select	Which statement supports . . . ?	
Show	What restrictions would you add?	
Summarize	Show in a graph, table.	
Tell		
Translate		

III. APPLY
(knowing when to apply; why to apply; and recognizing patterns of transfer to situations that are new, unfamiliar or have a new slant for students)

Verbs for Objectives	Model Questions	Instructional Strategies
Apply	Predict what would happen if . . .	Modeling
Choose	Choose the best statements that apply.	Cognitive apprenticeships
Dramatize	Judge the effects.	"Mindful" practice—NOT just a
Explain	What would result.	"routine practice"
Generalize	Tell what would happen.	Part and whole sequencing
Judge	Tell how, when, where, why.	Authentic situations
Organize	Tell how much change there would be.	"Coached" practice
Paint	Identify the results of . . .	Case studies
Prepare		Simulations
Produce		Algorithms
Select		
Show		
Sketch		
Solve		
Use		

IV. ANALYZE (breaking down into parts, forms)

Verbs for Objectives	Model Questions	Instructional Strategies
Analyze	What is the function of . . . ?	Models of thinking
Categorize	What's fact? Opinion?	Challenging assumptions
Classify	What assumptions?	Retrospective analysis
Compare	What statement is relevant?	Reflection through journaling
Differentiate	What motive is there?	Debates
Distinguish	Related to, extraneous to, not applicable.	Discussions and other collaborating learning activities

(Continued)

Figure 1.1 (Continued)

Verbs for Objectives	Model Questions	Instructional Strategies
Identify	What conclusions?	Decision-making situations
Infer	What does the author believe?	
Point Out	What does the author assume?	
Select	Make a distinction.	
Subdivide	State the point of view of . . .	
Survey	What is the premise?	
	What ideas apply?	
	What ideas justify the conclusion?	
	What's the relationship between?	
	The least essential statements are	
	What's the main idea? Theme?	
	What inconsistencies, fallacies?	
	What literacy form is used?	
	What persuasive technique?	
	Implicit in the statement is . . .	

V. EVALUATE (according to some set of criteria, and state why)

Verbs for Objectives	Model Questions	Instructional Strategies
Appraise	What fallacies, consistencies,	Challenging assumptions
Judge	inconsistencies appear?	Journaling
Criticize	Which is more important, moral better, logical, valid, appropriate?	Debates
Defend	Find the errors.	Discussions and other collaborating learning activities
Compare		Decision-making situations

VI. CREATE (SYNTHESIS)
(combining elements into a pattern not clearly there before)

Verbs for Objectives	Model Questions	Instructional Strategies
Choose	How would you test . . . ?	Modeling
Combine	Propose an alternative.	Challenging assumptions
Compose	Solve the following.	Reflection through journaling

Verbs for *Objectives*	*Model Questions*	*Instructional Strategies*
Construct	How else would you . . . ?	Debates
Create	State a rule.	Discussions and other
Design		collaborating learning activities
Develop		Design
Do		Decision-making situations
Formulate		
Hypothesize		
Invent		
Make		
Make up		
Originate		
Organize		
Plan		
Produce		
Role play		
Tell		
Tell		

Figure 1.1   Key Words, Model Questions, and Instruction Strategies

Compiled by the IUPUI Center for Teaching and Learning. Revised December 2002.

References

Anderson, L. W., & Krathwohl, D. R. (2001). *A taxonomy for learning, teaching, and assessing.*

Bloom, B. S. (Ed.). (1956). *Taxonomy of educational objectives. The classification of educational goals, by a committee of college and university examiners.* New York: Longmans.

John Maynard, University of Texas, Austin

Marilla Svinicki, University of Texas, Austin

REFLECTION AND APPLICATION

> How will I incorporate *brainstorming and discussion* to engage students' brains?

Standard/Objective: _____

_____

Activity: _____

_____

Standard/Objective: _____

_____

Activity: _____

_____

Standard/Objective: _____

_____

Activity: _____

_____

Standard/Objective: _____

_____

Activity: _____

_____

Standard/Objective: _____

_____

Activity: _____

_____

Standard/Objective: _____

_____

Activity: _____

_____

Standard/Objective: _____

_____

Activity: _____

_____

Strategy 2

Drawing and Artwork

WHAT: DEFINING THE STRATEGY

For more than 70 years, researchers (Allen, 2008; Dewey, 1934) have written about the positive relationship between thinking in art and thinking across the curriculum. Yet when school budgets become tight, the art program is one of the first thought to be expendable. Educators may need to think again. Case in point, the students enrolled in the performing arts school in the DeKalb County School System, where I worked for 30 years, have consistently had some of the highest test scores of any students in the district. Yet scoring high on tests was not one of the criteria for enrollment into the performing arts program. Could something else be at work here?

A person's ability to draw and design serves them well in the real world. Artists, architects, and interior designers are all paid well to use their unique abilities to transform the visual-spatial world around them. Yet in traditional classrooms, these talents are often perceived as interfering with instruction. I have seen students engaged in off-task behavior drawing imaginative cars, tennis shoes, superheroes, or celebrities of far greater interest than the boring lesson being taught in the front of the room.

Use the artistic creativity in students' brains to your cross-curricular advantage. Have them illustrate the definition of a vocabulary word in English, design a mural depicting all they remember from a previous lesson on the Civil War in history, draw the procedures involved in an experiment in science, or illustrate each step in a multistep word problem in mathematics. Those students who once saw no real correlation between what they would like to be in the real world (artists, sculptors, engineers) and what is happening in school may begin to rethink that relationship.

WHY: THEORETICAL FRAMEWORK

Drawing is a powerful way to develop the thought processes and perceptions of children. (Art Junction, n.d.)

Having students add drawings or doodles to their notes helps them comprehend and encode new content for later recall. (Allen, 2008)

Art helps students build self-esteem, develop their ability to solve problems, and improve manual dexterity and sensory awareness. (India Parenting, 2009)

When useful, teachers should encourage students to draw pictures that can help them gain more insight by representing abstract concepts graphically. (Posamentier & Jaye, 2006)

It is fun and simple to substitute art activities into any content area at any grade level in place of other activities. (Sousa, 2006)

Math books in Singapore teach students to draw models in an effort to visualize math problems prior to solving them. (Prystay, 2004)

The success of the mathematician and scientist is because of skills taken from the tools of the artist such as accurate observation, spatial thinking, and kinesthetic perception. (Sousa, 2006)

Different areas of the brain, including the amygdala and the thalamus, are activated when people are involved in art activities. (Jensen, 2001)

When children play—draw, dance, and sing—they engage every sense and help wire the neurons for learning successfully. (Sousa, 2006)

The use of patterns in art, music, dance, and drama assists the brain in its search for meaning. (Fogarty, 2001)

Thinking in art precedes improvements in thinking in other curricular areas. (Dewey, 1934)

HOW: INSTRUCTIONAL ACTIVITIES

WHO: Elementary/Middle/High
WHEN: During the Lesson
CONTENT AREA(S): All

• Give students an opportunity to create a personal *pictionary* by illustrating assigned content-area vocabulary words. Each page of the pictionary consists of an assigned word written in color, a drawing that depicts the meaning of the word, and an original sentence using the word in the appropriate context.

WHO: Elementary/Middle/High
WHEN: After the lesson
CONTENT AREA(S):   All

• To reinforce the concept of main idea or theme, have students design a book jacket or cover that depicts their understanding of the major idea of a book or story previously read.

WHO: Elementary/Middle/High
WHEN: During a lesson
CONTENT AREA(S):   Science

• Have students design a poster that illustrates the major details of a specific unit concept or unit of study. For example, students could illustrate one of the eight planets along with written pertinent facts regarding the planet.

WHO: Elementary/Middle/High
WHEN: During a lesson
CONTENT AREA(S):   Mathematics

• Give students a math word problem to read and then have them draw a series of pictures illustrating their understanding of what is actually happening in each step of the problem. Have them use the pictures to assist them in writing the numerical symbols for the word problem.

WHO: Elementary/Middle/High
WHEN: After a lesson
CONTENT AREA(S):   Science

• Have students draw and label a particular part or process of the human body, for example, the heart, lungs, digestive process, and so forth.

WHO: Elementary/Middle/High
WHEN: After a lesson
CONTENT AREA(S):   Social studies/history

• When students come in class, have a piece of butcher paper on one wall and markers available. Tell students that today they will design a class mural based on details that they remember from yesterday's class, such as, one thing they remember about the Civil War. Have them draw on their spot on the mural and be prepared to explain to the class what they drew and why. Then allow students to view one another's pictures, which should help in their recall of information.

WHO: Elementary/Middle/High
WHEN: After a lesson
CONTENT AREA(S):   Mathematics

• Have students make drawings that will illustrate mathematical terms that have already been taught. These could include such terms as, fraction, decimal, perpendicular lines, parallel lines, isosceles triangle, rhombus, radius, chord, and so forth.

WHO: Elementary/Middle/High
WHEN: During the lesson
CONTENT AREA(S): Music

• Give students paper with the bass and treble clef lines and spaces already drawn in. Have them draw in the notes to represent a simple or complicated piece of music. Assist them in connecting the musical notation to the actual notes played on a keyboard or other musical instrument.

WHO: Elementary/Middle/High
WHEN: After a lesson
CONTENT AREA(S): History

• To assist students in recalling information regarding a person or group of people, have them draw a stick person symbol. Have them attach notes about the person or group in eight areas to the appropriate spot on the figure: ideas to the brain, hopes or vision to the eyes, words to the mouth, actions to the hands, feelings to the heart, movement to the feet, weaknesses to the Achilles tendon, and strengths to the arm muscle (Sousa, 2006).

WHO: Middle/High
WHEN: During a lesson
CONTENT AREA(S): Mathematics

• Have students create tessellations to apply their understandings of symmetry and transformations. A tessellation is a pattern of shapes that is repeated over and over and covers a specific area. The repeated shapes must fit together with no overlaps or gaps. Use students' tessellations to teach concepts of area, angles, length, congruency, and transformation.

REFLECTION AND APPLICATION

How will I incorporate *drawing and artwork* into instruction to engage students' brains?

Standard/Objective: _____

_____.

Activity: _____

_____.

Standard/Objective: _____

_____.

Activity: _____

_____.

Standard/Objective: _____

_____.

Activity: _____

_____.

Standard/Objective: _____

_____.

Activity: _____

_____.

Standard/Objective: _____

_____.

Activity: _____

_____.

Standard/Objective: _____

_____.

Activity: _____

_____.

Strategy 3

Field Trips

WHAT: DEFINING THE STRATEGY

The purpose of the brain is not to make good grades or to score high on standardized tests. The brain has but one purpose—survival in the real world. Is it any wonder that the places that you travel to in the real world are long remembered? This would make the strategy of field trips one to be remembered.

Each year since she started teaching, my daughter Jennifer and I take her students on a field trip. It is not sponsored by the school. It is sponsored by us. Every year during one Saturday afternoon in December, Jennifer invites her students and any parents who wish to accompany us to dress up and meet us at the school. They then accompany us to a restaurant called The Spaghetti Factory. After a delicious and thrifty dinner, we all walk across the street to the historic Fox Theater and enjoy the Atlanta Ballet's production of *The Nutcracker*. Tickets are purchased in advance so that we all sit together and students get to experience a beautiful ballet. This will be the first time that many second or third-grade students have had such an experience and they never forget it. Many of her students come back years later recalling their time with Mrs. Clowers and her mother at the ballet.

I recall a comical instance during the first year when a student sitting next to me at the ballet tugged on my sleeve and asked this question, "When are they going to talk, Mrs. Tate?" He later realized that the *talking* is done with the feet.

WHY: THEORETICAL FRAMEWORK

Field trips enable students to better recall what they have learned because they escape the day-to-day classroom routine and see their education through the eyes of others. (Children's Health Education Center, n.d.)

Enhancing higher-order thinking skills, refining observation and questioning skills, raising a student's confidence and improving attitude are all benefits of taking field trips. (Children's Health Education Center, n.d.)

Taking students on field trips is one way to incorporate planned movement for learning content into the classroom. (Sprenger, 2007a)

Because students need concrete, real-world examples and need to see, touch, and experience the world, a field trip can be a useful teaching tool prior to starting a teaching unit. (Gregory & Parry, 2006)

Well-planned field trips are better than lab experiments in emulating good science because students formulate questions about nature, devise methods for answering the questions, implement the methods, evaluate the answers, and share the results with others. (Davis, 2002)

The classwork of adolescents should carry them into the "dynamic life of their environments." (Brooks, 2002, p. 72)

Enhancing higher-order thinking skills, refining observation and questioning skills, and increasing the confidence and attitude of students are all benefits of field trips. (Davis, 2002)

If students are to link their learning to prior knowledge, they must see the personal connection between what is being taught in the curriculum and their life experiences. (Lieberman & Miller, 2000)

Field trips, including those that are virtual, enable teachers to create as many authentic, experiential experiences as possible. These spatial memories are embedded in the brain and need no rehearsal. (Fogarty, 2001)

Concrete experience, not necessarily association, enables the brain to store a great deal of information. (Westwater & Wolfe, 2000)

When students get out of the classroom and into the real world, critical-thinking skills can improve. (Jensen & Dabney, 2000)

Aristotle and Socrates, two of the world's greatest teachers, used field trips thousands of years ago, as tools of instruction. (Krepel & Duvall, 1981)

HOW: INSTRUCTIONAL ACTIVITIES

WHO:	Elementary/Middle/High
WHEN:	Before a lesson
CONTENT AREA(S):	All

• Select a neighborhood or community site for the class to visit that will reinforce a curricular objective. Plan for the class to visit the site prior to instruction in the unit so that students will experience real-world images that will help them clarify concepts when the unit is taught.

WHO:	Elementary/Middle/High
WHEN:	Before a lesson
CONTENT AREA(S):	All

• For a change of scenery, convene class outside on the school grounds. Allowing students to experience the positive effects of sunlight and the beauty of nature calms students' brains and puts the mind in a good state for learning. Conducting a class discussion while sitting under a tree can add a whole new dimension to instruction.

WHO:	Elementary
WHEN:	During a lesson
CONTENT AREA(S):	Mathematics

• Use the school as well as the community for your field trip. Ask students to look for patterns in their environment such as in the stars and stripes on the American flag, clothing of classmates, the brick in the school building, or the leaves on the trees. Point out the obvious way that objects, shapes, and colors are patterned in the real world.

WHO:	Elementary/Middle/High
WHEN:	After an assignment
CONTENT AREA(S):	Mathematics

• Take students on a walk around the school or school grounds. Have them stop when they see a geometric shape in the real world that you have taught in class: the circular bark of a tree, the rectangular wall of the school, the octagonal shape of a stop sign, the angles on the basketball court.

WHO:	Elementary/Middle
WHEN:	After a lesson
CONTENT AREA(S):	Science

• Prior to a unit of study on the solar system, have students visit a planetarium where they actually see replicas of what they will be studying including the stars, planets, constellations, and so forth.

WHO: Elementary
WHEN: During a lesson
CONTENT AREA(S):   History

- Plan and take a field trip to a natural history or other type of museum to view exhibits and artifacts related to a unit of study. Visit the museum in advance and plan a scavenger hunt so that when students visit they can search for predetermined items and find the answers to pre-arranged questions.

WHO: Elementary/Middle
WHEN: During a lesson
CONTENT AREA(S):   Mathematics

- Have students find coupons in the newspaper reflecting an amount of savings on five of their favorite foods. As a homework assignment, have students actually take a trip to the grocery store and find the selected items. They then calculate what percentage of the total cost was saved by using the coupons.

WHO: Elementary/Middle/High
WHEN: After a lesson
CONTENT AREA(S):   All

- Oftentimes, the classroom does not provide enough space for movement and games. Take the class outside and engage them in purposeful movement to reinforce a content objective or to play a game that requires more space than four walls will allow.

WHO: Middle/High
WHEN: During a lesson
CONTENT AREA(S):   Mathematics

- Have students walk around their community and create math problems from their environment based on what they are discovering as they walk around the neighborhood. Have them accompany their problems with the photographs, videos, or recordings essential for others to solve the problem. Submit your students' best math problems, along with the accompanying visuals to the National Math Trails Web site. These problems are then posted to the appropriate grade level for students throughout the United States to solve.

WHO: Elementary/Middle/High
WHEN: During a lesson
CONTENT AREA(S):   All

- Students can now experience what it is like to visit other locations of interest and never leave the classroom. Go online to appropriate Web sites and access virtual field trips that pertain to a concept being taught.

REFLECTION AND APPLICATION

> How will I incorporate *field trips* into instruction to engage students' brains?

Standard/Objective: _____

_____

Activity: _____

_____

Standard/Objective: _____

_____

Activity: _____

_____

Standard/Objective: _____

_____

Activity: _____

_____

Standard/Objective: _____

_____

Activity: _____

_____

Standard/Objective: _____

_____

Activity: _____

_____

Standard/Objective: _____

_____

Activity: _____

_____

Strategy 4

Games

WHAT: DEFINING THE STRATEGY

In the name of increased academic achievement, school systems are removing recess time from the students' school day. Yet there is a saying that goes as follows: *You don't stop playing because you get old. You get old because you stop playing.* While prekindergarten children love to play games, it is also one of the 10 activities that keep people living beyond the age of 80 (Mahoney, 2005). That would lead one to believe that games are beneficial throughout one's life and that elementary, middle, and high school students would benefit from spirited interaction in the pleasurable strategy of game playing. Boys, especially, are naturally motivated when a review is turned into a competition.

My family and I are constantly involved in game playing. My two daughters, son-in-law, and I are all evenly matched in our ability to play *Scrabble.* Many great evenings have been spent making words that are ripe for a challenge! My husband and I play Backgammon, and he enjoys a spirited game of chess. We have a whole game corner in our house and love to engage family members in Taboo, Pictionary, or Scattergories.

Games can be just as useful in the classroom. Not only is the strategy motivating but it also can put students' brains in a positive state. When students are engrossed in game playing, the stress is lessened and memory for content is increased!

WHY: THEORETICAL FRAMEWORK

Using game formats encourages students to cooperate with one another, helps them focus and pay attention, and is motivating and loads of fun. (Algozzine, Campbell, & Wang, 2009a)

When students develop a game's content as well as play the game, the amount of time they are exposed to and involved with the content is doubled. (Allen, 2008)

Games are not only perfect for raising the level of feel-good amines in the brain but also, in the correct amounts, games can also increase cognition and working memory. (Jensen, 2007, p. 4)

Games such as *Wheel of Fortune* and *Jeopardy* provide students with great formats for remembering content. (Caine, Caine, McClintic, & Klimek, 2005)

A ball-toss game not only encourages cooperation, problem solving, and physical movement but it also enables students to think and act quickly while operating in a safe environment. (Jensen, 2007)

With very little practice, students enjoy writing questions for one another to be used when playing a game. (Caine et al., 2005)

Children playing outside in the neighborhood not only learn formal rules but also the informal concepts of camaraderie, negotiation, cooperation, and physical skills. (Jensen, 2007)

Using an event in history, a model, or a game to explore the richness of math are some of the various ways teachers can discover new ways to teach specific math topics. (Posamentier & Hauptman, 2006)

When students perceive their learning environment as positive, endorphins are produced that stimulate the frontal lobes of the brain and give students a feeling of euphoria. (Sousa, 2006)

Students not only learn more when playing a game but their participation in class and their motivation for learning math increases. (Posamentier & Jaye, 2006)

When students are stressed and perceive their learning environment as negative, cortisol is produced, which interferes with the recall of emotional memories. (Kuhlmann, Kirschbaum, & Wolf, 2005)

When those students who are going to play the game actually construct it, the game becomes more effective. (Wolfe, 2001)

The need for survival, belonging and love, power, freedom, and fun are the five critical needs that must be satisfied if people are to be effectively motivated. (Glasser, 1999)

HOW: INSTRUCTIONAL ACTIVITIES

WHO:	Elementary/Middle/High
WHEN:	After a lesson
CONTENT AREA(S):	All

- Buy a generic game board, such as *Candy Land,* with a starting and a finishing point. Have students play in pairs or in small groups. Make game cards to review an objective that has already been taught. Each student in the group takes turns rolling a die or spinning a spinner and then moving their marker along the game board the same number of spaces rolled. However, to move the rolled number of spaces, students have to pick the same number of cards and identify the concept on each card. For every concept correctly identified, the student moves one space. The first student in each team to get to the end of the game is the winner.

WHO:	Elementary/Middle/High
WHEN:	After the lesson
CONTENT AREA(S):	All

- Have students work in cooperative groups to construct an original game board according to the following guidelines: The game must provide at least 30 spaces, including a *begin* and *end* space, two *move ahead* spaces, and two *go back* spaces. Have students make game question cards appropriate to whatever content needs to be reviewed with an accompanying answer key. Each group of students uses another group's game board and questions. Each group reviews content by rolling a number generator (die), moving the rolled number of spaces, selecting a card, and answering the designated question on the card. If the answer is correct, the student moves the rolled number of spaces. If the answer is incorrect, the student stays put. The first student in each group to get to the end of the game board wins.

WHO:	Elementary/Middle/High
WHEN:	During the lesson
CONTENT AREA(S):	All

- Have students make 15 matched pairs of content-area vocabulary words and their definitions. Have them write each word on one index card and the accompanying definition on another card. Have them spread the word and definition cards out facedown in random order. Students work in pairs taking turns matching each word to its appropriate definition. One match entitles the student to another try. The student with the most matches at the end of the game wins.

WHO:	Elementary/Middle
WHEN:	During the lesson
CONTENT AREA(S):	Mathematics

• Have students work in pairs to become more automatic with addition facts. Give each pair a deck of cards. Have students deal the deck equally between the two of them. Have each student hold their half deck in their hand with the cards facedown. Have them turn the top cards up simultaneously and add the value of the two cards together. For example, if one student turns over a 7 and another a 3, then the first student to say 10 gets both cards. Jacks are worth 11 points; Queens are worth 12 points; and Kings are worth 13 points. Aces can be worth either 1 point or 14 points. The first student to take all the cards or the one who has the most cards when the time is up is named the winner. You may want to pair students with like abilities together.

WHO: Elementary/Middle/High
WHEN: After the lesson
CONTENT AREA(S):   All

• Write each content-area vocabulary word on a different index card. Have students play *Charades* by taking turns coming to the front of the room, selecting a word card, and acting out the definition of the word. The student is not allowed to speak or write but must use gestures to act out the word. The first student in class to guess the word gets a point. The student with the most points at the end of the game is the winner.

WHO: Elementary/Middle/High
WHEN: After the lesson
CONTENT AREA(S):   All

• Play *Jeopardy* with the class by dividing them into three heterogeneous teams. Each team selects a team captain who gives the answers to the emcee and a scribe who keeps track of the points for the team and writes down the *Jeopardy* answer during the bonus round. Select key points from the chapter or unit of study and turn them into answers for the board. Five answers are placed into five columns of $100 increments with the easiest answers worth $100 and the most difficult worth $500. Teams then compete against one another by taking turns selecting an answer and providing the appropriate question. If the answer is correct, the points are added to the score. If the answers are incorrect, the points are subtracted. Include two *daily doubles* to make the game more interesting. Play continues according to the rules of the television show until all of the answers have been selected. Any team with money can wager any or all of it during the *bonus round*. The team with the most money at the end of the game wins.

WHO: Elementary/Middle/High
WHEN: After the lesson
CONTENT AREA(S):   All

• Play *Wheel of Fortune* with the class by selecting a content-area vocabulary word previously taught. Place one line on the board for each letter in the chosen word. Have students take turns guessing letters of the alphabet that may be in the word. If the letter is in the word, write it on the correct line. If it is not, place the letter in a column off to the side. The first student to guess the word wins a point.

Adaptation: Have students work in pairs to select a word and have their partner guess the word. The student in each pair who guesses their word in the shortest amount of time is the winner.

WHO:	Elementary/Middle/High
WHEN:	During the lesson
CONTENT AREA(S):	All

- Have students participate in a *People Search* where they have to find answers to 12 short, unfinished statements in a 4 × 3 grid drawn on a piece of paper. The statements should reflect content that you would like for students to review. Students can supply only one answer for themselves. Then they must get the remaining 11 answers from 11 different classmates. Play some fast-paced music and have students walk around the classroom getting answers from their peers. As each peer provides an answer, they initial each student's paper indicating that they provided the answer. At the end of the song, students should have 12 different initials including their own and the answers to all 12 statements. Review the statements with the entire class to be sure that all students have the correct answers.

WHO:	Elementary/Middle/High
WHEN:	During the lesson
CONTENT AREA(S):	All

- Have students play the *Loop* game by writing the statements and questions similar to the following on index cards and passing them out randomly to students in the class. Students then use the cards to answer one another's questions.
  - o **I have a right triangle.** Who has a triangle with all sides congruent?
  - o **I have an equilateral triangle.** Who has the number of degrees in each of its angles?
  - o **I have 60 degrees.** Who has the segment of a triangle from a vertex to the midpoint of the opposite side?
  - o **I have median.** Who has a triangle with each angle less than 90 degrees?
  - o **I have an acute triangle.** Who has a triangle with at least two congruent sides?
  - o **I have an isosceles triangle.** Who has an equation whose graph is a line?
  - o **I have a linear equation.** Who has the name of the side opposite the right angle in a right triangle?
  - o **I have the hypotenuse.** Who has an equation for the area of a circle?
  - o **I have a = πr^2.** Who has an equation that states that two ratios are equal?
  - o **I have proportion.** Who has a quadrilateral with four congruent sides?

Students can write additional questions and answers that will form the basis of the remaining cards for playing this game. You should have as many cards as there are students in class (Bulla, 1996).

Adaptation: This game can be adapted to any content area by changing the answers and the questions.

WHO: Elementary/Middle/High
WHEN: During the lesson
CONTENT AREA(S):   All

• Provide students with a bingo sheet containing 25 blank spaces. Have students write previously taught, content-area vocabulary words randomly in any space on their cards. Then have students take turns randomly pulling from a bag and reading the definition of a designated word. Have students cover or mark out each word as the definition is read. The first student to cover five words in a row, horizontally, vertically, or diagonally, shouts out, "Bingo!" However, to win, the student must orally give the definition for the five words that comprise the *bingo*. If the student cannot supply the definitions, then play continues until a subsequent student wins.

Adaptation: Have students randomly write answers to math problems in the 25 blank spaces. Have students randomly pull and read math problems from the bag as students cover the correct answers.

WHO: Elementary/Middle/High
WHEN: During the lesson
CONTENT AREA(S):   Language arts/History

• Have students play the *Who Am I?* game by providing written clues regarding a famous literary or historical figure already studied. Have students take turns reading their clues aloud as class members try to guess the identity of the figure. Any student who is the first to guess wins a point. If no one is able to identify the figure, then the student providing the clues gets the point.

WHO: Elementary/Middle/High
WHEN: After the lesson
CONTENT AREA(S):   All

• Have students compete in pairs and take turns being the first to get their partners to guess a designated vocabulary word by providing them with a one-word synonym or clue for the word. No gestures are allowed. Bring two pairs to the front of the class. One pair begins. The point value begins at 10 and decreases by one each time the word is not guessed. This game is patterned after the television game show *Password*.

WHO: Elementary/Middle/High
WHEN: During the lesson
CONTENT AREA(S):   All

• During a class discussion, when a question is asked, toss a Nerf or any other soft ball to the student who is to respond. The student gets one point for catching the ball and two points for answering the question correctly. If the student is correct, he or she can randomly pick the student who is to answer the next question and randomly toss the ball to that student. If the student answers incorrectly, he or she must toss the ball back to you so that you can select the next student. Be sure to ask the question of the entire class prior to selecting someone to catch the ball and answer the question.

WHO:	Elementary/Middle/High
WHEN:	After the lesson
CONTENT AREA(S):	All

• Following a unit of study and prior to a test, have students work in heterogeneous groups to write 10 questions regarding the content at varying levels of difficulty with four possible answer choices. Each question is assigned a monetary level of difficulty in $100 increments ranging from $100 to $1,000. Have them also write three additional difficult questions worth $5,000, $25,000, and $100,000, respectively. Have student groups compete to earn money for their team by answering another team's questions. This game is adapted from the television game show, *Who Wants to Be a Millionaire?*

WHO:	Elementary/Middle/High
WHEN:	During the lesson
CONTENT AREA(S):	All

• Encourage students to review appropriate content-area vocabulary by playing *Pictionary.* Divide the class into two heterogeneous teams. Students from each team take turns coming to the front of the room, pulling a vocabulary word from a box, and drawing a picture on the board that will get their team members to say the word before time is called. No words may be spoken. If the team succeeds in guessing the word within a specific time limit (such as 30 seconds), the team gets one point. The team with the most points when all words have been used is the winner.

WHO:	Elementary/Middle/High
WHEN:	During the lesson
CONTENT AREA(S):	All

• Purchase the CD, *Classic TV Game Show Themes,* so that you have the music that accompanies many of the games that you will play with your class. The CD has the themes from the following game shows: *Wheel of Fortune, Jeopardy, Password, Family Feud, The Price is Right,* and many more.

WHO:	Elementary/Middle
WHEN:	During the lesson
CONTENT AREA(S):	All

• Consult the series *Engage the Brain Games* for a plethora of additional game ideas across the curriculum. Books for grade levels kindergarten through Grade 5 are cross-curricula, including games in the content areas of language arts, math, science, social studies, music, and physical education. There is a separate book in each of the following four content areas: language arts, mathematics, science, and social studies, for Grades 6 through 8.

REFLECTION AND APPLICATION

How will I incorporate *games* into instruction to engage students' brains?

Standard/Objective: _____

_____

Activity: _____

_____

Standard/Objective: _____

_____

Activity: _____

_____

Standard/Objective: _____

_____

Activity: _____

_____

Standard/Objective: _____

_____

Activity: _____

_____

Standard/Objective: _____

_____

Activity: _____

_____

Standard/Objective: _____

_____

Activity: _____

_____

Strategy 5

Graphic Organizers, Semantic Maps, and Word Webs

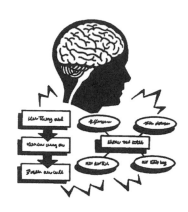

WHAT: DEFINING THE STRATEGY

Whether referred to as concept, mind, or semantic maps or as word webs or graphic organizers, these tools are some of the best friends of a teacher who desires to facilitate the comprehension of students. They address both the left and the right hemispheres of students, so they are beneficial to all. The students strong in left hemisphere can supply the verbage, and the right-hemisphere students have the option of showing what they know pictorially. Have students draw the organizer along with you as you explain the major concepts and details.

When I teach my class *Worksheets Don't Grow Dendrites,* a picture of a neuron serves as a graphic organizer or mind map for the five elements of a brain-compatible classroom. The main ideas are in boxes and the details are written underneath. Main ideas and details are color-coded. See the diagram below. By the time I have finished teaching this part of the class, teachers know that the best classrooms are ones where students are actively engaged in the learning—talking to one another, moving to learn content, connecting ideas together, thinking positively, and having a purpose for the learning.

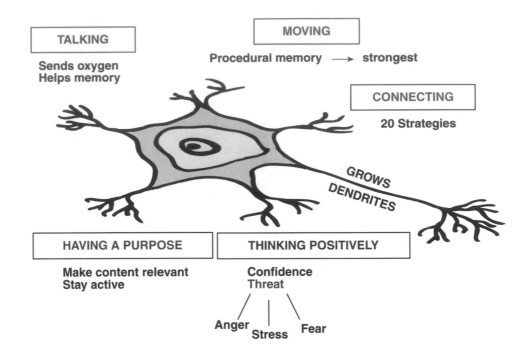

TALKING

Sends oxygen
Helps memory

MOVING

Procedural memory ⟶ strongest

CONNECTING

20 Strategies

GROWS DENDRITES

HAVING A PURPOSE

Make content relevant
Stay active

THINKING POSITIVELY

Confidence
Threat

Anger   Stress   Fear

WHY: THEORETICAL FRAMEWORK

Graphic organizers are effective tools for supporting thinking and learning in four major ways: (1) abstract information is represented in a concrete format, (2) relationships between facts and concepts are depicted, (3) new information is connected to previous knowledge, and (4) thoughts are organized for writing and for problem solving. (Ronis, 2006)

Graphic organizers, scaffolding, and activating prior knowledge are techniques that are research proven to help teachers better connect with students. (Deshler & Schumaker, 2006)

Graphic organizers represent a form of nonlinguistic representation and are one of the most popular ways teachers can have students represent the knowledge that they have experienced. (Marzano, 2007, p. 52)

The models and mental maps that students produce prior to a unit of study enable teachers to correct misunderstandings and expand on their prior knowledge. (Jensen, 2007)

Mind mapping, a very special form of imagery, combines pictures with language to assist students in seeing how concepts are related to other concepts and how they connect to a main idea. (Sousa, 2006)

Having students create a mind or concept map is a meaningful strategy for helping them make sense of and learn vast amounts of new content. (Budd, 2004)

Graphic organizers not only gain the attention of students but can also improve comprehension, meaning, and retention. (Sousa, 2007)

Frustration can be avoided when teachers allow students to structure their ideas into the easily understood format that an original mind map can provide. (Goldberg, 2004)

Because the brain remembers images more easily than just words, graphic organizers are one of the tools that are effective for organizing patterns. (Feinstein, 2004)

Graphic organizers enable English learners to organize words and ideas in a way that helps them see patterns and relationships in mathematics. (Coggins, Kravin, Coates, & Carrol, 2007)

Concept maps, a type of graphic organizer, integrate both visual and verbal activities and enhance comprehension of concrete, abstract, verbal, and nonverbal concepts. (Sousa, 2006)

Graphic organizers are powerful tools for instruction since they enable students to organize data into segments or chunks that they can comprehend and manage. (Gregory & Parry, 2006, p. 198)

Flow charts, continuums, matrices, Venn diagrams, concept maps, and problem-solution charts are all types of graphic representations that can be used by mathematics teachers because they can be quickly understood and can provide structure for synthesizing new information. (Posamentier & Jaye, 2006)

When graphic organizers are used to change words into images, both left- and right-brain learners can use those images to see the big picture. (Gregory & Parry, 2006)

HOW: INSTRUCTIONAL ACTIVITIES

WHO:	Elementary/Middle/High
WHEN:	Before and after the lesson
CONTENT AREA(S):	All

• To access students' prior knowledge and summarize content after a lesson is taught, have students complete a K-N-L graphic organizer. Have students discuss or brainstorm (1) what they already *know* about a concept or unit of study; (2) what they will *need* to know to comprehend the concept, and (3) following instruction, what they have *learned*.

K-N-L Graphic Organizer		
Topic:		
What I Know	What I Need to Know	What I Learned

WHO: Elementary/Middle/High
WHEN: During the lesson
CONTENT AREA(S):   All

• Because the brain thinks in chunks or connections, have students increase their knowledge of vocabulary by using a word web. As new vocabulary is introduced, have students complete the word web below by brainstorming additional synonyms for the new word. Students can keep their word webs in a notebook for review and add synonyms throughout the year. Encourage them to add these words to their speaking and writing vocabularies as well.

Word Web

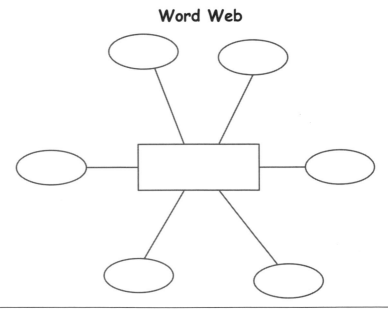

WHO:	Elementary/Middle/High
WHEN:	After the lesson
CONTENT AREA(S):	All

- After the reading of a story or novel where problems exist that must be resolved, have students complete the following story frame to demonstrate their understanding of the story's plot.

Story Map

Title: _____

Setting: [box]

Characters: _____   _____
              _____   _____
              _____   _____

[box]

Problem:
Event 1 _____
Event 2 _____
Event 3 _____
Event 4 _____

[box]

Solution

WHO:	Elementary/Middle/High
WHEN:	During the lesson
CONTENT AREA(S):	All

- To help students identify the main idea and details in narrative or content-area texts, have them complete the following graphic organizer. It will assist students in understanding that supporting details should add up to the main idea.

Main Idea/Details

Details

Main Idea

WHO: Elementary/Middle/High
WHEN: During the lesson
CONTENT AREA(S): All

• Have students identify cause-effect relationships in narrative and content-area texts by completing the graphic organizer below. This will help them understand that every action has an accompanying effect.

Cause/Effect

So

WHO: Elementary/Middle/High
WHEN: During the lesson
CONTENT AREA(S): All

• Have students complete the following graphic organizer to demonstrate their understanding of a character's traits and to site evidence in narrative or expository texts to support the given traits.

Character Traits

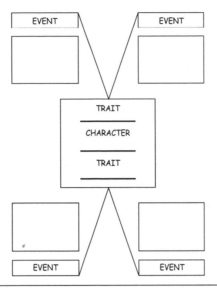

WHO: Elementary/Middle/High
WHEN: During the lesson
CONTENT AREA(S): All

• Have students complete the following graphic organizer to identify sequence of events and to show how one event leads to another in either narrative or content-area texts.

Sequence

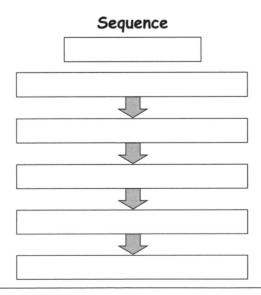

WHO:	Elementary/Middle/High
WHEN:	During the lesson
CONTENT AREA(S):	All

• Have students compare and contrast two or more characters or events in narrative or content-area texts by using the following Venn diagram.

Compare/Contrast

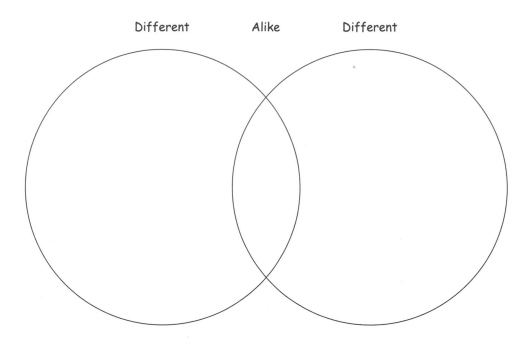

Different   Alike   Different

WHO:	Elementary/Middle/High
WHEN:	During the lesson
CONTENT AREA(S):	All

• While lecturing or discussing ideas with students, complete a semantic, concept, or mind map on the board to show how the major concepts are related to one another. Have students copy the map in their notes as you explain each part. See a sample format below.

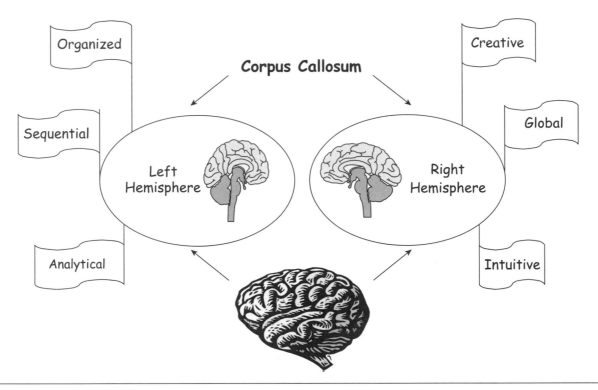

WHO: Elementary/Middle/High
WHEN: After the lesson
CONCEPT AREA(S):   All

• Once you have demonstrated how to do so, encourage students to create their own semantic, concept, or mind maps regarding a unit of study. This technique alone will enhance comprehension because these mind maps can be reviewed prior to testing to facilitate long-term retention.

WHO: Elementary/Middle
WHEN: Before, during, and after the lesson
CONCEPT AREA(S):   All

• Refer to the series *Engage the Brain: Graphic Organizers and Other Visual Strategies* to find additional graphic organizers in the content areas of language arts, math, science, and social studies. Grades K–5 have all content areas contained in the same book. Grades 6–8 have separate books for each of the four content areas. Consult the Corwin Web site at www.corwin.com for information.

REFLECTION AND APPLICATION

How will I incorporate *graphic organizers* into instruction to engage students' brains?

Standard/Objective: _____

_____

Activity: _____

_____

Standard/Objective: _____

_____

Activity: _____

_____

Standard/Objective: _____

_____

Activity: _____

_____

Standard/Objective: _____

_____

Activity: _____

_____

Standard/Objective: _____

_____

Activity: _____

_____

Standard/Objective: _____

_____

Activity: _____

_____

Strategy 6

Humor

WHAT: DEFINING THE STRATEGY

Two older couples were enjoying friendly conversation at dinner when one gentleman asked the other, Fred, "How was that memory clinic you went to last month?" Fred replied, "The memory clinic was wonderful! They used the latest techniques with us. They told us stories. They taught us with metaphors. It was simply great and helped me tremendously!" The first man asked, "Fred, what was the name of the clinic? I may need to go because my memory is giving me problems." Fred thought and he thought, but he could not remember the name of the clinic. Then about 30 minutes later, a smile broke across Fred's face, and he asked, "What do you call that flower with the long stem and the thorns?" The other gentleman looked puzzled, but he asked, "Fred, are you talking about a rose?" Fred replied, "I'm not sure, but I think that's it." Then he turned to his wife and asked, "Rose, what was the name of that memory clinic I attended?"

If that joke made you laugh or even smile, it put your brain in a more positive state. Research (Allen, 2008; Jensen, 2007) shows that jokes, riddles, celebrations, and other forms of positive interaction not only create a positive learning environment but may also facilitate the learning itself. Did you know that the brain does not know the difference between real laughter and fake laughter? You can fake laughter and it will have the same positive effect on the brain. That is *why there are more than 1,800 laughing clubs in India alone.*

Please do not confuse the use of humor in the classroom with sarcasm, which has the exact opposite effect on the brains of students. The literal definition of sarcasm is *a tearing of the flesh,* aptly named because remarks directed to students that demean, tease, or deride can, at minimum, hinder or incapacitate higher-level thinking (Jensen, 1995).

WHY: THEORETICAL FRAMEWORK

"What we learn with pleasure, we never forget." (Allen, 2008, p. 99)

Improvisational comedy enables students to think on their feet, puts a bit of fun and laughter into a lesson, and encourages students to take risks in front of their peers. (Udvari-Solner & Kluth, 2008)

Having laughter breaks in class increases the flow of positive neurotransmitters, which are necessary for alertness and memory. (Jensen, 2007)

Effective classrooms are alive with positive emotion, anticipation of novel experiences, the excitement of discovery, and celebrations of success. (Allen, 2008)

Humor has been found to free a person's creativity and to foster higher-level thinking skills, such as perceiving and anticipating novel situations, creating visual images, and forming analogies. (Costa, 2008)

Having students set and achieve personal goals, such as learning their multiplication tables, helps them build on their successes and savor memories of positive feelings. (Willis, 2007)

The periodic use of humor in class helps the teacher provide a sense of cooperation and concern. (Gettinger & Kohler, 2006)

Because laughter increases the endorphin level in the body, lowers the heart rate and the stress hormone, cortisol, students in a laughing classroom are more likely to take risks and tend to be more creative and collaborative. (Gregory & Parry, 2006)

More than 30 years ago, researchers found that the most effective teachers at the junior high level smiled a great deal and had a tendency to joke with students. (Moskowitz & Hayman, 1976)

Play is essential in helping children practice those social skills essential for everyday life. (McCormick Tribune Foundation, 2004)

When students are experiencing minimal stress, levels of cognition are increased and information is allowed to flow more freely through the amygdala, the seat of emotion. (Willis, 2007)

Older adolescents are more apt to understand the subtleties of humor, satire, or irony since their language skills are more highly developed than those of younger students. (Feinstein, 2004)

The use of humor is 1 of 12 intelligent behaviors, labeled as *habits of mind*. These *habits* are based on the premise that all students can be taught a set of skills that enable them to behave in intelligent ways. (Costa, 1991)

HOW: INSTRUCTIONAL ACTIVITIES

WHO:　　　　　　　　Elementary/Middle/High
WHEN:　　　　　　　 Before a lesson
CONTENT AREA(S):　　All

• Have teachers in a grade level or a department form a laughing club. There are more than 1,800 such clubs in India, and because the brain does not know the difference between real laughter and fake laughter, they appear to work. The laughing club can meet before school long enough for a teacher to share a joke or riddle with the members. Teachers can take turns bringing the jokes for the week. Everyone gets his or her day off to a positive start that can carry over into instruction.

WHO: Middle/High
WHEN: Before, during, or after a lesson
CONTENT AREA(S): All

• Almost every middle and high school classroom has a *class clown.* Use that student to your advantage. Have them bring in jokes and/or riddles to tell to the class. Make sure you approve of each joke before it is shared. Either before class, during the last few minutes, or at appropriate times during the period, have the class clown tell a joke. The entire class will laugh putting each brain in a positive state for learning. The job of the class clown can rotate to other volunteers in the class each week until every student who wants a turn has had one.

WHO: Elementary/Middle/High
WHEN: During a lesson
CONTENT AREA(S): All

• Locate or create and incorporate cartoons, riddles, and jokes that reinforce concepts to be taught into the delivery of instruction.

WHO: Middle/High
WHEN: After the lesson
CONTENT AREA(S): All

• Have students create original jokes regarding a concept previously taught. The creation of jokes not only reinforces students' conceptual understanding but also encourages students to use their higher-level thinking skills.

WHO: Middle/High
WHEN: Before or during a lesson
CONTENT AREA(S): All

• Have students bring in riddles to share with the class. Read over each riddle and place the ones you approve in a *riddle box.* At the beginning of class or periodically throughout the period, stop and read a riddle from the box. Give points to the first student who can come up with the answer. The student who brought in the riddle is not allowed to guess but gets points for bringing in the riddle and extra points if no student can come up with the answer in a given time.

WHO: Elementary/Middle/High
WHEN: After the lesson
CONTENT AREA(S):   All

- Use humorous ways to randomly involve students in lessons. When students are working in cooperative groups and it is time to select a spokesperson for the group, have students point into the air. Then, on the count of three, have them point to the person in their group they want to be the spokesperson. The student with the most fingers pointing at him or her becomes the spokesperson. This activity always gets a hearty laugh!

WHO: Elementary/Middle/High
WHEN: Before the lesson
CONTENT AREA(S):   All

- Select students to fulfill a variety of roles in cooperative groups according to humorous categories such as the following:
    - Students wearing red (or any other color)
    - Students wearing contacts or glasses
    - Students wearing jewelry, such as rings or earrings
    - Students who have the most brothers, sisters, or pets
    - Students who live closest to or farthest from school

WHO: Middle/High
WHEN: After the lesson
CONTENT AREA(S):   All

- Have students design original cartoons, comic books, or super-heroes to illustrate a key concept previously taught. For example, students could design a comic book where the main character is *Preposition Man,* a superhero with all the strengths and powers of this part of speech.

WHO: Middle/High
WHEN: During the lesson
CONTENT AREA(S):   All

- Locate editorial or other cartoons that emphasize cross-curricular concepts already taught. Display them in class and have students use their higher-level thinking skills to explain the concept displayed in the cartoon. For older students, you may want to display the cartoon omitting the caption and have students work individually or in groups to create their own captions. You would be surprised how your students' originals captions may be superior to the ones provided in the cartoons.

WHO: Elementary/Middle/High
WHEN: After the lesson
CONTENT AREA(S):   All

• Play games with students to review content prior to a test. Consult Chapter 4: Games for numerous examples for involving students in a fun class with lots of humor.

WHO: Elementary/Middle/High
WHEN: During the lesson
CONTENT AREA(S):   All

• Provide positive feedback for appropriate student responses in humorous ways, such as providing applause with a plastic hand clapper, sending positive energy with a *positive energy stick* (magic wand), or blowing a paper horn.

WHO: Elementary/Middle/High
WHEN: During the lesson
CONTENT AREA(S):   All

• Have students support and celebrate appropriate answers given by peers. These might include, but are not limited to, the following:

   o Applause
   o Thumbs-up
   o High fives
   o Original cheers
   o Standing ovations

Consult Chapter 17: Celebrations of the book, *Shouting Won't Grow Dendrites: 20 Techniques for Managing a Brain-Compatible Classroom* for more than 25 additional ways to celebrate student success in the classroom.

WHO: Elementary/Middle/High
WHEN: Before the lesson
CONTENT AREA(S):   All

• To create an environment conducive to optimal learning, place humorous signs around the room. For example, one sign could say, *Knowledge given away here, free. Bring your own container* (Burgess, 2000, p. 20).

REFLECTION AND APPLICATION

How will I incorporate *humor* into instruction to engage students' brains?

Standard/Objective: _____

_____.

Activity: _____

_____.

Standard/Objective: _____

_____.

Activity: _____

_____.

Standard/Objective: _____

_____.

Activity: _____

_____.

Standard/Objective: _____

_____.

Activity: _____

_____.

Standard/Objective: _____

_____.

Activity: _____

_____.

Standard/Objective: _____

_____.

Activity: _____

_____.

Strategy 7

Manipulatives, Experiments, Labs, and Models

WHAT: DEFINING THE STRATEGY

My daughter Jennifer is a teacher and a wonderful teacher she is! In fact, this year she is Teacher of the Year for her school. Jen and I still remember when she took chemistry in 10th grade. As I followed her progress during the semester, I noticed the 100% average that she achieved on every laboratory assignment. However, when I attended a conference with her chemistry teacher, I was told that she was not faring as well on her paper and pencil tests. You see, Jen's lab grade only constituted 10% of her overall semester average. The more I thought about what real chemists do, such as lab work, the more questions I had. For example, if the major job of school is to prepare students for success in the real world, and real chemists conduct labs most of the time, then why does lab work only count for 10% of the grade in a chemistry class? How many students have given up any hope of being a chemist because their inadequate grades reflected more their grade on written tests than their ability to conduct experiments in the real world? After all, when is the last time a chemist walked into the laboratory, sat down, and completed a worksheet or took a paper and pencil test?

My son, Christopher, had difficulty paying attention in class when his teachers lectured for the majority of the period. However, this was the same person who, as a teenager, could spend hours in his room constructing a moving ferris wheel out of *K'nex* blocks or who excelled in a summer hands-on science camp sponsored by Georgia Institute of Technology.

Two of my three children, and many others like them, probably possess what Howard Gardner (1983) called visual-spatial intelligence.

These students usually excel with hands-on strategies, such as the use of manipulatives, conducting experiments, and constructing models, and teachers would do well to incorporate this strategy into their repertoire.

WHY: THEORETICAL FRAMEWORK

Teachers should provide students with manipulatives and have students engaged in holding and molding clay or other objects. (Jensen, 2008)

When students are working with concrete shapes, they are developing the foundation for spatial sense. (Wall & Posamentier, 2006)

Students' understanding of mathematical ideas is broadened when concrete representations are used. (Coggins, Kravin, Coates, & Carrol, 2007)

Manipulatives are valuable resources for assisting even high school students in accelerating their mathematics ability. (Curtain-Phillips, 2008)

When learning is active and hands-on, the formation of neural connections is facilitated and information is much more readily remembered than information learned from an abstract viewpoint, where the teacher is doing the work while the students watch. (Gregory & Parry, 2006)

Because concrete materials assist English language learners in focusing on new concepts and vocabulary at the same time, they are a crucial part of the instruction in fluency with mathematics. (Coggins et al., 2007)

When students use manipulatives over a long period, they make gains in verbalizing their thinking, discussing ideas, taking ownership, and gaining confidence in independently finding answers to problems. (Sebesta & Martin, 2004)

Manipulatives provide a strong foundation for students mastering concepts in measurement, decimals, percentages, probability, statistics, and number relations. (Access Center, 2004)

The use of the hands and brain activity are so complicated and interconnected that no one theory explains it. (Jensen, 2001)

Students in the early grades should be allowed to use manipulatives for as long as the students feel they are needed. (Checkley, 1999)

HOW: INSTRUCTIONAL ACTIVITIES

WHO: Elementary/Middle/High
WHEN: During the lesson
CONTENT AREA(S):   Mathematics

• Place manipulatives, such as tiles, blocks, or Cuisenaire rods, on the document camera as you teach so students have a visual example of how they can use manipulatives to demonstrate a concept being taught.

WHO:	Elementary/Middle/High
WHEN:	During the lesson
CONTENT AREA(S):	Mathematics

• Have students use manipulatives, such as Unifix cubes, tiles, blocks, Cuisenaire rods, miniature clocks, or geoboards, during mathematics instruction to display their understanding of a particular concept taught.

WHO:	Elementary/Middle/High
WHEN:	During the lesson
CONTENT AREA(S):	Science

• Design a laboratory experiment for students and allow them to follow specific directions to complete the experiment, demonstrating their understanding of a science concept being taught.

WHO:	Elementary
WHEN:	During the lesson
CONTENT AREA(S):	All

• Have students practice spelling or content-area vocabulary words in a number of tactile ways including the following: writing the words in the air, writing them in shaving cream spread on the desk (a side benefit of this activity is that you end up with a clean desk when the activity ends), forming the words with clay or other pliable materials, or using magnetic alphabet letters to build the words.

WHO:	Elementary/Middle/High
WHEN:	During the lesson
CONTENT AREA(S):	History

• Bring in artifacts and have students bring in artifacts as well for them to handle and observe as you discuss a certain period of history.

WHO:	Elementary/Middle/High
WHEN:	During the lesson
CONTENT AREA(S):	All

• Have students construct models that show their understanding of a concept previously taught. For example, have students construct a model of the solar system that shows the planets in order from the sun—from Mercury to Neptune or have students construct a model of a home to scale with all of the necessary rooms and fixtures.

WHO:	Elementary/Middle/High
WHEN:	During the lesson
CONTENT AREA(S):	Mathematics

• Give students pieces of construction paper and ask them to place the pieces in the shape of a pizza. Some students have two pieces, some four pieces, and some have eight pieces, all which form a whole pizza. Have students assemble the pieces of their pizza and then compare the sizes of their pieces with other classmates. Ask them to make assumptions regarding the sizes of the pieces, becoming familiar with terms such as halves, fourths, and eighths.

Adaptation: Instead of a pizza, give students a hamburger with all of the condiments cut out of round circles. The burger is on brown construction paper and is divided into halves, the cheese on top is on yellow paper and is in thirds, the red tomato is in fourths, the green pickle is in fifths, and the white onion is in sixths. The hamburger is set between two buns and enables students to see that although each part of the hamburger is in different fractional pieces, each piece adds up to the whole circle.

WHO: Elementary/Middle/High
WHEN: During the lesson
CONTENT AREA(S):   All

• Have students use their hands to show agreement or disagreement with an answer or level of understanding for an answer by doing one of the following:

  o Thumbs-up if you agree
  o Thumbs-down if you disagree
  o Five fingers if you completely understand
  o One finger if you don't understand
  o Pat head if you understand
  o Scratch head if you don't understand

WHO: Elementary
WHEN: During the lesson
CONTENT AREA(S):   Mathematics

• Students can use their fingers as a human calculator for the nine times tables. Have students hold their hands up in front of them (palm side facing away from the body) and spread their fingers. Starting with the little finger on the left hand, have students assign a number to each finger. When multiplying using the nine times tables, have them turn down the finger that represents the number to be multiplied times nine. For example, if the student is multiplying nine times four, then the fourth finger on the left hand is turned down. All fingers to the left of the turned down finger is the first digit in the answer and all fingers to the right of the turned down finger is the second digit in the answer. Therefore, the answer to $9 \times 4 = 36$.

REFLECTION AND APPLICATION

How will I incorporate *manipulatives, experiments, labs, and models* into instruction to engage students' brains?

Standard/Objective: _____

_____

Activity: _____

_____

Standard/Objective: _____

_____

Activity: _____

_____

Standard/Objective: _____

_____

Activity: _____

_____

Standard/Objective: _____

_____

Activity: _____

_____

Standard/Objective: _____

_____

Activity: _____

_____

Standard/Objective: _____

_____

Activity: _____

_____

Strategy 8

Metaphors, Analogies, and Similes

WHAT: DEFINING THE STRATEGY

Of all 20 strategies, this one is probably one of the most effective. Because the brain is a *maker of meaning,* it is constantly searching for connections and patterns. Students can understand many new and complicated concepts when those concepts are compared to dissimilar ones that the students already know and understand.

For example, when I teach the concept of *main idea* to elementary students, I tell them that a main idea and details are like a table and legs. The top of the table is the main idea and the legs are the supporting details. Just like the legs hold up the top of the table, the main idea *holds up* or supports the main idea in a story or written composition. We then draw a table and as we read, we write the main idea on the table and one detail from the story on each leg. When students write a composition without enough support for the main idea of a paragraph, all I have to do is say, "Your table is leaning." They know exactly what I mean!

Middle and high school students are best taught main idea by comparing the concept to a text message. I tell them that when you send someone a text message, you have to give them just the gist. To give someone many details is too expensive. Like the text message, the main idea gives the gist. A funny story happened when I was teaching a sixth-grade class in Los Angeles and related the aforementioned comparison. A student raised her hand and said the following: "Mrs. Tate, my text messages aren't expensive; we have the family plan." So much for my simile!

WHY: THEORETICAL FRAMEWORK

When students use metaphor and analogy, two "semantic transformations," to explain a concept, content becomes more coherent. (Jensen, 2009a, p. 56)

Metaphor uses the familiar to explain something unfamiliar and describes the conceptual using something tangible. (Jones, 2008)

Creating metaphors and creating analogies are two of the four types of tasks students should use to identify similarities and help them develop knowledge. (Marzano, 2007)

When students connect what they are learning in mathematics with other content areas, math is viewed as more useful and interesting than when math is taught as a separate subject. (Posamentier & Jaye, 2006)

Using analogies to clarify or explain ideas assists students in making pertinent connections and increasing their comprehension of content. (Gregory & Parry, 2006)

Teachers who give students analogies when providing explanations have students who are capable of conceptualizing complex ideas. (Posamentier & Jaye, 2006)

Metaphors can be used for both content and skill instruction because they are full of imagery and can convey meaning as well and as rapidly as literal language. (Sousa, 2006)

Metaphor allows one to examine a concept from a broader perspective, such as how it applies across the curriculum, to the real world of the student, or to life as a whole. (Allen, 2002)

Making metaphorical connections stretches students' thinking and increases their understanding. (Gregory & Chapman, 2002)

Having students classify, compare, contrast, and use analogies and metaphors increases their achievement because they can look for similarities and differences between ideas or things. (Marzano, Pickering, & Pollack, 2001)

The majority of concepts are understood only in relation to other concepts. (Lakoff & Johnson, 1980)

HOW: INSTRUCTIONAL ACTIVITIES

WHO: Elementary
WHEN: During the lesson
CONTENT AREA(S):   Language arts

- To introduce the concept of *simile*, read aloud the book *I'm as Quick as a Cricket* by Audrey Wood. Read it the first few times simply for enjoyment. Then have students think of ways they are like animals. Help them write a story using the following pattern: *I'm as* _____*as a* _____. Compile their stories into a class book.

WHO:	Elementary/Middle/High
WHEN:	During the lesson
CONTENT AREA(S):	All

- Whenever possible, introduce a new or difficult concept by comparing it to a concept that students already know and understand. For example, in French the word "rouge" means red, which is similar to the makeup "rouge" that some women wear. When teaching the layers of the earth's sediment, have students compare those layers to the dirty clothing deposited in a laundry basket. The most recent deposits would be on the top in both instances.

WHO:	Elementary/Middle/High
WHEN:	During the lesson
CONTENT AREA(S):	Mathematics

- Assist students in understanding that certain operations in math are analogous to other operations. Help them to see that addition and subtraction are simply inverse operations, as are multiplication and division. Show them that multiplication is simply a faster form of addition. Because the brain is constantly searching for connections, consistently demonstrating these relationships to students should help them to better understand and apply these concepts.

WHO:	Elementary/Middle/High
WHEN:	During the lesson
CONTENT AREA(S):	All

- To assist students in comprehending the relationship between two concepts in any content area, have them create analogies. Give them the pattern a : b :: c : d (a is to b as c is to d) to show how two sets of ideas or concepts are related. For example, Shakespeare : *Hamlet* :: Charles Dickens : *A Christmas Carol* or Eli Whitney : the cotton gin :: Thomas Edison : the light bulb. Once they get the hang of it, students can then create their own analogies, leaving a blank line for other students to complete.

WHO:	Elementary/Middle/High
WHEN:	After the lesson
CONTENT AREA(S):	Music

- Assist students in seeing the analogous relationship between types of notes in music and fractions in math. For example, in 4/4 time, it takes two half notes, four quarter notes, and eight eighth notes to make a whole note. Similarly, it takes, 2/2, 4/4, and 8/8 also make a whole. Have students write musical notation to symbolize fractional parts.

WHO:	Elementary/Middle/High
WHEN:	During the lesson
CONTENT AREA(S):	All

• Have students pretend to be detectives and look for metaphors, analogies, and similes in narrative and expository texts. Post a list of the examples students find, and periodically, ask students to explain the relationships that exist between the two concepts. Add to the list throughout the year.

WHO:	Elementary/Middle/High
WHEN:	During the lesson
CONTENT AREA(S):	Language arts

• As students write, have them create metaphors that improve the quality of their writing and symbolize their understanding of the relationship between two unrelated concepts. Have them explain the relationship to a partner. For example, students could write the following: *Life is a journey. The brain is a computer.*

WHO:	Elementary/Middle/High
WHEN:	During the lesson
CONTENT AREA(S):	All

• To encourage creative thinking, have students complete a cloze sentence such as the following: If ____ were a ____, it would be ____ because ____. For example, if *the brain* were *a piece of jewelry*, it would be a *chain* because *it has many links.*

WHO:	Elementary/Middle/High
WHEN:	During the lesson
CONTENT AREA(S):	History

• To understand that history repeats itself, help students connect current events to similar events that happened in the past. For example, students could compare the current recession with the Great Depression that occurred years earlier. Have them use a Venn diagram to compare and contrast how the two periods are alike and how they are different. Consult Strategy 5 for a model of a Venn diagram.

REFLECTION AND APPLICATION

How will I incorporate *metaphors, analogies, and similes* into instruction to engage students' brains?

Standard/Objective: _____
_____.

Activity: _____
_____.

Standard/Objective: _____
_____.

Activity: _____
_____.

Standard/Objective: _____
_____.

Activity: _____
_____.

Standard/Objective: _____
_____.

Activity: _____
_____.

Standard/Objective: _____
_____.

Activity: _____
_____.

Standard/Objective: _____
_____.

Activity: _____
_____.

Standard/Objective: _____
_____.

Activity: _____
_____.

Strategy 9

Mnemonic Devices

WHAT: DEFINING THE STRATEGY

When I teach the workshop that accompanies this book, I always give my participants a way to remember my name so that they will never forget me—even if they don't see me for another 10 years. Because my first name is Marcia and the brain looks for connections, I use the television show of *The Brady Bunch* as my connection. You may remember that the oldest daughter's name was Marcia. Marcia had a younger sister named Jan who was envious of her because Marcia got all of the attention as the oldest. The connection I give them for remembering the spelling of my name is actually a mnemonic device. Instead of my mother spelling my name *M-a-r-s-h-a*, she spelled it *M-a-r-c-i-a*, which means I am called *Mar-ci-a (Mar-see-a)* all the time. But to remember the spelling, I tell them that I am a member of the CIA. It always works! I run into teachers who have not seen me for years and who will greet me with *Hi, Marcia from the CIA!*

Acrostics and acronyms are examples of mnemonic devices and they serve as effective tools for remembering. In fact, the word itself derives from the Greek word *mnema*, which means memory. Mnemonics devices used in the real world to help the public remember include *acquired immune deficiency syndrome (AIDS)* or *sudden infant death syndrome (SIDS)* and we are all familiar with the *Internal Revenue Service (IRS)*.

Mnemonics can be just as valuable in your classroom. When students are given the word "HOMES" to remember the Great Lakes of **H**uron, **O**ntario, **M**ichigan, **E**rie, and **S**uperior, or the sentence "**E**very **G**ood **B**oy **D**oes **F**ine" for the notes on the treble clef in music, test scores and memory increase.

WHY: THEORETICAL FRAMEWORK

Learning is increased twofold to threefold when people rely on mnemonic devices rather than their regular learning habits. (Markowitz & Jensen, 2007)

Mnemonic techniques are time-tested activities that enable students to recall and use material without conscious effort from the brain. (Mayer, 2003)

An acronym turns a recall task into an "aided recall task" because students are remembering chunks of information rather than a lot of information at one time. (Allen, 2008, p. 16)

Acrostics can serve as triggers to help students recall content, but students may need help connecting the acrostic to the material. (Allen, 2008)

Process mnemonics, such as PEMDAS (**P**lease **E**xcuse **M**y **D**ear **A**unt **S**ally), are very effective for students having difficulty in math because they are attention-getting, motivational, and actively engage the brain in processes essential to learning and memory. (Sousa, 2007)

Retention and recall are improved when students are provided with a mnemonic aid. (Ronis, 2006)

Regular people can greatly increase memory performance with mnemonic devices because they can be useful for recalling unrelated information, rules, or patterns. (Sousa, 2006)

Mathematics instruction is more relevant and cohesive when mnemonics are used to link abstract symbols with concrete associations. (Bender, 2005)

Mnemonic devices benefit students but are more meaningful when the students create their own rather than memorize those provided by the teacher. (Feinstein, 2004)

Mnemonic devices should be used only after students have had an opportunity to thoroughly process the information, even if their understanding is incomplete. (Marzano, 2007)

HOW: INSTRUCTIONAL ACTIVITIES

WHO: Elementary/Middle/High
WHEN: During the lesson
CONTENT AREA(S):   All

• To assist students in recalling content previously taught and thoroughly processed, create acrostics (acronyms and acrostics), which will help them remember. Teach these mnemonic devices, and use them consistently during instruction so students hear them multiple times and can use them to recall content during and after tests.

WHO: Elementary/Middle/High
WHEN: During the lesson
CONTENT AREA(S):   All

• Have students create their own acrostics to assist them in remembering content. For example, one teacher had students create original acrostics to remember the order of operations in math. Students will remember best what they choose to create themselves, especially if the mnemonic devices are humorous or novel. For example, instead of the customary *Please Excuse My Dear Aunt Sally* (**P**arentheses, **E**xponents, **M**ultiply, **D**ivide, **A**dd, **S**ubtract) one student created the following original acrostic: *Please End My Day At School.*

WHO: Elementary/Middle/High
WHEN: During the lesson
CONTENT AREA(S):   Mathematics

• To help eliminate the threat that occurs in the brain when some students lack confidence in their ability to be successful in your math class, teach them the acronym that Connie Moore of Los Angeles California uses MATH, which actually stands for **M**ath **A**in't **T**hat **H**ard! I know that the word "ain't" is not grammatically correct, but this acronym is too good to overlook. If you use the 20 strategies as you teach, you can watch this acronym come true.

WHO: Elementary/Middle/High
WHEN: During the lesson
CONTENT AREA(S):   All

• To recall a series of items, have students use *chunking* as a mnemonic device by linking items together with meaningful and memorable associations. For example, students can remember the following number by making associations: 1492007200025 becomes Columbus sailed the ocean blue in (1492) with James Bond (007) at the turn of the century (2000) for a generation (25 years).

WHO: Elementary/Middle/High
WHEN: During the lesson
CONTENT AREA(S):   All

• Have students look for examples of mnemonic devices in narrative and expository texts. Post a list of examples and review them periodically to facilitate memory.

WHO: Elementary/Middle/High
WHEN: During the lesson
CONTENT AREA(S):   All

• After being given numerous examples, have students create phrases or slogans to help them understand and remember information that is difficult to recall. For example, *30 days hath September, April, June, and November . . .* helps one to recall the number of days in each month.

WHO: Elementary/Middle/High
WHEN: During the lesson
CONTENT AREA(S):   All

• Mnemonic devices are used in the real world consistently to help the public remember content that would be otherwise difficult to recall. Have students look for examples of mnemonic devices in the real world, such as SCUBA, CIA, or FBI and bring their list to class. Post a list of real-life examples and see how many the class can come up with in a combined list.

WHO: Elementary/Middle/High
WHEN: During the lesson
CONTENT AREA(S):   Mathematics

• To help students comprehend the text of a word problem, use the *SQRQCQ* strategy, which serves as a mnemonic device:

Survey: Obtain a general understanding of the problem by reading it quickly.

Question: Find out what information is required in the problem.

Read: Read the problem again to find information that is relevant to solving the problem.

Question: Ask what operations must be performed and in which order to solve the problem.

Complete: Do the computations necessary to get a solution.

Question: Ask whether the answer is reasonable and the process complete.

WHO: Elementary/Middle/High
WHEN: During the lesson
CONTENT AREA(S):   All

• Have students use the *peg-word system* and linking to remember items in order. Have them associate a rhyming word with each number 1 through 10. For example, 1 = bun, 2 = shoe, 3 = tree, 4 = door, 5 = hive, 6 = sticks, 7 = heaven, 8 = gate, 9 = sign, and 10 = hen. Have them then link each item on the list with the designated rhyming word in the most absurd visual possible. For example, if the second item on the grocery list is lettuce, have students visualize the lettuce in a shoe (2) to recall that lettuce is the second thing on the list.

REFLECTION AND APPLICATION

| How will I incorporate *mnemonic devices* into instruction to engage students' brains? |

Standard/Objective: _____

_____

Activity: _____

_____

Standard/Objective: _____

_____

Activity: _____

_____

Standard/Objective: _____

_____

Activity: _____

_____

Standard/Objective: _____

_____

Activity: _____

_____

Standard/Objective: _____

_____

Activity: _____

_____

Standard/Objective: _____

_____

Activity: _____

_____

Strategy 10

Movement

WHAT: DEFINING THE STRATEGY

Recently, I watched the National Spelling Bee champion on the nightly news. They showed footage as she was spelling her winning word, which, by the way, was one I could not begin to pronounce or spell. Before she spelled the word, she wrote it with her finger on her opposite hand. I thought to myself, "Whoever coached her really knows the brain research." You see, her coach knew that she would have an easier time recalling the spelling of multiple words if those words were placed in procedural or muscle memory. Procedural memory is one of the strongest memory systems in the brain and is the reason that one seldom forgets how to drive a car, ride a bicycle, play the piano, type on a keyboard, tie one's shoes, or brush one's teeth. It is accessed when the body is involved while one is learning. When there is a brain-body connection, memory is enhanced.

In many traditional classrooms, students sit for long periods in uncomfortable desks, and if they get up, they are chastised for being out of their seats. One teacher commented to me that we spend the first three years of our students' lives teaching them to walk and talk and the next 15 telling them to *"Sit down!"* and *"Shut Up!"* Rather than having students watching you as you move around the classroom, have them up and moving along with you. Not only does it strengthen memory and decrease behavior problems but also it makes teaching and learning so much fun! When I go in to teach a model lesson, I always incorporate some type of movement. Students often comment about the amount of fun they are having and ask whether I can return to teach another lesson on the next day. Of course, I can't because I am off to conduct another class or teach a workshop in another place.

WHY: RESEARCH RATIONALE

Dance is not only a form of communication but also it improves attention to detail and can assist students with sequencing and thinking logically. (Karten, 2009)

Any task learned when we are physically engaged in doing it remains in our memory for a very long time. (Allen, 2008)

Physical performance is probably the only known cognitive activity that uses 100 percent of the brain. (Jensen, 2008)

Movement provides an external stimulus to match an internal stimulus and, therefore, reinforces memory. (Markowitz & Jensen, 2007)

Movement triggers memory because the basal ganglia and cerebellum, once thought to be only associated with controlling muscle movement, have been found to be important in coordinating thought processes as well. (Markowitz & Jensen, 2007)

Because physical movement increases the energy of students, it, therefore, enhances their engagement. (Marzano, 2007)

Procedural or muscle movement strengthens memory because it triggers the production of glucose and involves more neurons than simple tasks that do not involve movement. (Paulin, 2005)

Physical movement sends more oxygen and nutrients to the brain and increases the production of nerve growth factor and dopamine, a neurotransmitter that enhances mood. (Jensen, 2008)

Movement not only assists with reading, gets blood and glucose to the brain, changes the state or mood of the brain, and provides lots of fun during learning but it also assists with our strongest memory system—procedural memory. (Sprenger, 2007b)

Instructional situations that involve the use of movement necessitate more sensory input than do situations requiring only paper and pencil. (Gregory & Parry, 2006)

Repeat a movement often enough and that movement becomes a permanent memory. (Sprenger, 2007a)

Movement not only enhances learning and memory but it also causes neural connections to become stronger. (Hannaford, 2005)

The brain fuels itself on the oxygen in the blood, which is produced by physical activity. (Sousa, 2001)

A change of stimuli is crucial because the amount of time a student can focus is equivalent to the age of the student in minutes. (DeFina, 2003)

The one most detrimental barrier to learning and recall of information may be a teacher's deliberate attempt to stop students from moving. (Jensen, 2002)

HOW: INSTRUCTIONAL ACTIVITIES

WHO:	Elementary/Middle/High
WHEN:	During the lesson
CONTENT AREA(S):	All

• Have students select or assign students an *energizing partner*, another student in the classroom who sits at a distance. Both students are provided with opportunities to stand and meet with one another to discuss any assigned task, such as reteaching a concept just taught by the teacher (Gregory & Chapman, 2002).

WHO:	Elementary/Middle/High
WHEN:	During the lesson
CONTENT AREA(S):	All

• Rather than having students always raise their hand if they agree with an answer provided by a classmate, have them stand if they agree and remain seated if they disagree. Standing provides more blood and oxygen throughout the body and keeps your students more alert.

WHO:	Elementary/Middle/High
WHEN:	During the lesson
CONTENT AREA(S):	All

• Have students take turns standing and reading short passages aloud in a choral response. Because students are reading together, those students who may be struggling can still participate and will hear the passage read correctly by others. Make this activity more fun by having students read while standing on one foot, holding their paper in the air, reading without taking a breath, and so forth.

WHO:	Elementary
WHEN:	After the lesson
CONTENT AREA(S):	Language arts

• Using the children's book *A, My Name is Alice* by Jane Bayer (1984), reinforce initial consonant sounds by having students jump rope as each verse is read by the teacher or recited by the students. For example, the second verse reads as follows:

B, My name in Barbara.

And my husband's name is Bob.

We come from Brazil.

And we sell balloons.

Barbara is a BEAR.

Bob is a BABOON.

Students can make up their own rhymes and then jump rope to their original rhymes. This book not only reinforces initial consonant sounds but also introduces students to different kinds of animals and their natural habitats.

WHO: Elementary/Middle
WHEN: During the lesson
CONTENT AREA(S):   Language arts

• To help students distinguish between common and proper nouns, use the following activity. Compile a list containing both common and proper nouns taken from content previously covered in class. Read each word aloud. Have students stand when a proper noun is called and remain seated when a common noun is called.

WHO: Elementary/Middle/High
WHEN: During the lesson
CONTENT AREA(S):   Music

• Have students sit in chairs that represent the lines (EGBDF) on the treble clef. Other students stand in spaces between the chairs and represent the spaces (FACE) on the treble clef. When a note is called out or played on an instrument, have students stand if seated or squat, if standing, if their position on the scale corresponds to the note played. Once they are familiar with the treble clef notes, engage them in the same activity using the lines and spaces on the bass clef.

WHO: Elementary
WHEN: During the lesson
CONTENT AREA(S):   Mathematics

• Have the entire class skip count aloud by 2s, 3s, 5s, 10s, 20s, and so on. Add movement by having them clap or take turns jumping rope while skip counting.

WHO: Elementary/Middle/High
WHEN: Before the lesson
CONTENT AREA(S):   All

• Have students draw the *appointment clock* on their paper. Put on fast-paced music and have students move around the classroom making appointments with four students in class, one appointment for 12 o'clock, a different student for 3 o'clock, a different one for 6 o'clock, and a final student for 9 o'clock. Have them write each student's name on the corresponding line. Then, as you teach lessons throughout the day or week, have students keep their appointments by discussing content with one another or reteaching a concept previously taught.

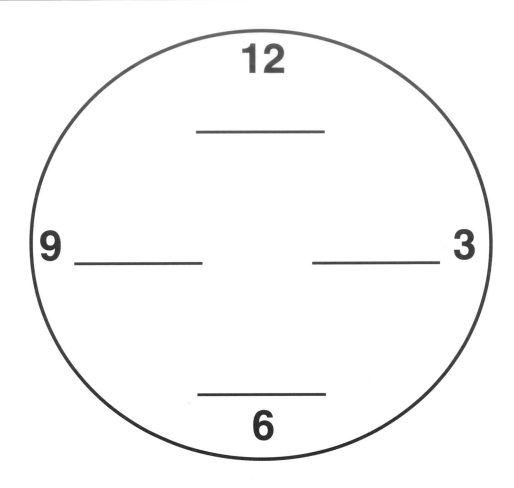

WHO: Elementary/Middle/High
WHEN: Before the lesson
CONTENT AREA(S):   All

• Have students draw a *seasonal appointment clock* on their paper. Put on fast-paced music and have students move around the classroom making appointments with four students in class, one appointment for fall, a different student for winter, a different one for spring, and a final student for summer. Have them write each student's name on the corresponding line. Then, as you teach lessons throughout the day or week, have students keep their seasonal appointments by discussing content with one another or reteaching a concept previously taught.

WHO: Elementary/Middle/High
WHEN: During the lesson
CONTENT AREA(S):   Mathematics

• Engage students in the *circumference conga* to teach students the concepts of *circumference, radius,* and *diameter*. Have all students in class form a circle. Stand in the middle of the circle. Have them do the conga by putting their hands on the shoulders of the person in front of them and moving to the salsa music. The circle represents the *circumference*. When you say, "Turn," have them reverse the circle. Then say, "freeze" and the circle stops. Then

Seasonal Dates

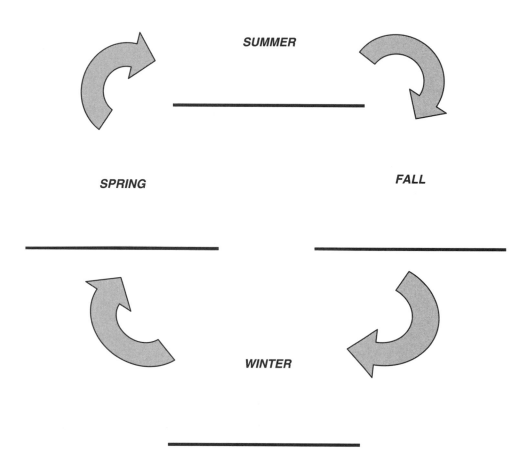

SUMMER

SPRING

FALL

WINTER

point to a student in the circle and appoint them as the *radius.* The radius then dances (or walks) over to you and then back to their original position (because the radius only extends to the center of the circle). The circle (circumference) then moves again. Say, "freeze." Then point to a different student in the circle who can be the *diameter.* The diameter dances (walks) over to you and then straight to the opposite side (because the diameter goes all the way through the circle). Repeat this dance for as long as you desire. Gloria Estefan's song "Conga" is the perfect music for this activity.

WHO: Elementary/Middle/High
WHEN: During the lesson
CONTENT AREA(S):   All

• When teaching sequential order (such as events in history, action in a story, or steps in the scientific process), put the separate events or steps on index cards and then pass them out to students in class. Put on fast-paced music, such as the theme from *The Price Is Right,* and have students place themselves in sequential order before the music ends. Then have the class decide if students have placed themselves correctly.

WHO: Middle/High
WHEN: During the lesson
CONTENT AREA(S):   Mathematics

- Have students do the *number line hustle*. Draw a number line on the board. Explain the position of the positive and negative integers on the number line. Have students stand and tell them that they will be doing the number line hustle by moving along the number line. Have each student stand in a place in the room where they have space to move to the left and to the right. They should all be facing in the same direction, preferably turned toward the number line on the board. You may use any appropriate disco music, such as Van McCoy's "The Hustle." Put on the music and then position yourself in front of the class. Lead the class in the movements necessary to solve the following problems:

(Problem I: $+5 + -3 = ?$) Have students move with you to the music five steps in a positive direction ($+5$). Then have them move three steps in a negative direction (-3). Ask them what number they landed on. The class should say $+2$.

Ask the class what they would have to do to get back to zero. (They should say move two steps in a negative direction.) Have them move back to zero.

(Problem II: $-6 + +10 = ?$) Starting at zero, have students move six steps in a negative direction (-6). Then have them move $+10$ steps in a positive direction. Ask the class, "What number are you on?" ($+4$)

Have the class sit down. Put the same problems that you danced out on the board so that students can see the connection between the concrete and the abstract. Then provide five additional problems for students to work either individually or in pairs. Give students the option of going to the back of the classroom and dancing along the number line to solve the additional problems while the music continues to play softly in the background.

REFLECTION AND APPLICATION

How will I incorporate *movement* into instruction to engage students' brains?

Standard/Objective: _____

_____

Activity: _____

_____

Standard/Objective: _____

_____

Activity: _____

_____

Standard/Objective: _____

_____

Activity: _____

_____

Standard/Objective: _____

_____

Activity: _____

_____

Standard/Objective: _____

_____

Activity: _____

_____

Standard/Objective: _____

_____

Activity: _____

_____

Strategy 11

Music, Rhythm, Rhyme, and Rap

WHAT: DEFINING THE STRATEGY

Denise, a teacher in Livingston, Tennessee, related a story to me that I will not soon forget. Not too many months after Hurricane Katrina devastated parts of New Orleans, Denise and four other adults took 40 teenagers to the ravaged area to assist in the clean-up effort. Four van loads of people headed for New Orleans. Denise had taken my *Worksheets Don't Grow Dendrites* class where we talked about the power of music on the brain, so she decided that while she was driving her 10 teenage passengers, she would be playing her CDs titled, *700 Hours of the World's Most Beautiful Classical Music*. While her teenage passengers did not necessarily want to be entertained in this way, they reluctantly agreed because they had formed a relationship with Denise and wanted to ride in her van. She even decided that whenever the caravan stopped to eat, her passengers could listen to whatever they wanted on their iPods, but while she was driving, only classical music could be played. Every time the cars stopped, the other three drivers were stressed. The teenagers in their vans were complaining, arguing with one another, and asking how much longer the trip would take. Denise remarked that every person in her van spent his or her time sleeping. They slept all the way to New Orleans and all the way back. That is the effect classical music has on the state of the brain, even the teenage brain!

Two other relationships regarding music and the brain have to do with its effect on memory and its relationship to mathematical ability. Whenever students put content to music, they stand a better chance of remembering it. Some research (Allen, 2008; Sousa, 2006) also suggests that the same spatial part of the brain that is activated when one is playing a musical instrument or sight reading music is also activated when one is solving higher-level math problems. Some Japanese parents in my workshops have shared that they enroll their young children in Suzuki violin lessons realizing the possible correlation between their musical ability and their academic achievement.

WHY: THEORETICAL FRAMEWORK

Music has the remarkable ability to energize, relax, set the daily mood, stimulate student brains, inspire, and make the learning fun. (Jensen, 2009a)

Students at all levels of education benefit when teachers create rhymes from the content but an even more effective technique may be having students create the rhymes themselves. (Allen, 2008)

Teachers who incorporate music in their classrooms have the benefit of a second teacher in the classroom—one who manages the students' emotional states. (Jensen, 2008)

The critical ingredient for improving the performance of students on spatial tasks is musical rhythm. (Jensen, 2007)

Musical intelligence does not live in one place in the brain because it is connected to the spatial and emotional intelligences and definitely tied to logical and sequential skills as well. (Kagan & Kagan, 2007)

Having students create songs of information to be memorized in rounds or in parts adds more fun and variety to the learning. (Caine, Caine, McClintic, & Klimek, 2005)

The tempo, beats per minute, of the music affects the breathing and heartbeat of students—two things that determine their state, mood, or feelings. (Jensen, 2009a)

Music has the capability to increase the body's molecular and muscular energy, lessen the body's pain and stress, speed up the healing process, and stimulate reasoning, thinking, memory, creativity, and intelligence. (Jensen, 2008)

Classical music by composers like Mozart and Beethoven stimulate beta waves in the brain and is appropriate for students to use when brainstorming or problem solving. (Sprenger, 2007b)

There is evidence that some types of music actually boost intelligence. After just 10 minutes of listening, some Mozart compositions have assisted students in increasing their intelligence scores on tests of spatial-temporal reasoning. (Jensen, 2007)

Of all the content areas, mathematics appears to be the one most closely aligned with music. Music uses ratios, proportions and fractions for tempo, patterns for notes or chords, counting for beats and rests, and geometry for placement of the fingers on a guitar. (Sousa, 2006)

Fast music with 100 to 140 beats per minute can be energizing for the brain while calming music at 40 to 55 beats per minute can be relaxing. (Jensen, 2005)

Certain musical selections from the baroque period have fewer beats per minute and encourage the brain to calm down and relax. (Sprenger, 2007a)

The rhythms, contrasts, and patterns of music help the brain encode new information, which is why students easily learn words to new songs. (Jensen, 2005; Webb & Webb, 1990)

Change the music during a learning episode. Set an emotional mood before class starts, upbeat tunes for moving around the room, music appropriate to the task during seatwork, and positive music at the end of the class. (Sousa, 2006)

The mathematics scores of low socioeconomic students more than doubled for those who took music lessons compared to those who did not. (Catterall, Chapleau, & Iwanga, 1999)

HOW: INSTRUCTIONAL ACTIVITIES

WHO:	Elementary/Middle/High
WHEN:	Before or after a lesson
CONTENT AREA(S):	All

• To maximize instructional time and minimize transition time, play music. Music with approximate beats of 50 to 70 per minute line up with the heart and calm the brain. This music can include classical, jazz, New Age, Celtic, Native American music, or nature sounds. Have this type music playing as students enter your room to help to ensure appropriate behavior for the beginning of class.

WHO:	Elementary/Middle/High
WHEN:	Before or after a lesson
CONTENT AREA(S):	All

• Rather than calming music, oftentimes high-energy music is the order of the day. Music with beats of 110 to 160 per minute energizes the brain and body and can bring excitement to your lesson. This type of music can include salsa, rhythm and blues, rock and roll, and fast-paced country/western.

WHO:	Elementary/Middle/High
WHEN:	Before, during, and after
CONTENT AREA(S):	All

• Review content with students using rock, rap, or country/western CDs from the company *Rocknlearn*. Each CD comes packaged with a book and can be found at a local teacher store or by logging on to www.rockn learn.com.

WHO:	Elementary/Middle/High
WHEN:	During a lesson
CONTENT AREA(S):	All

• Find appropriate music to accompany your lesson and incorporate it directly into your teaching. For example, Billy Preston's "Will It Go Round in Circles" is perfect for teaching circumference in math and Billy Joel's "We Didn't Start the Fire" can accentuate your history lesson.

WHO:	Elementary/Middle/High
WHEN:	Before, during, and after
CONTENT AREA(S):	All

• Music can change the state of students' brains. Consult books that can assist you with your selection of music such as Eric Jensen's *Top Tunes for Teaching* or Rich Allen's *The Ultimate Book of Music for Learning*. Listed below are some of my favorite artists and selections that I use when teaching both students and adults.

Emile Pandolfi—classical pianist

- *An Affair to Remember*
- *By Request*
- *Days of Wine and Roses*
- *Secret Love*
- *Some Enchanted Evening*

Kenny G.—jazz

- *At Last . . . The Duet's Album*
- *The Ultimate Kenny G.*

Artists' Greatest Hits

- *Best of Hiroshima*
- *Doobies*
- *Earth, Wind and Fire: Greatest Hits*
- *Greatest Hits:* Gloria Estefan
- *Hits:* Phil Collins
- *Song Review: A Greatest Hits Collection* (Stevie Wonder)
- *Sounds of Summer* (Beach Boys)
- *Stardust . . . The Great American Songbook: Vol. III* (Rod Stewart)
- *Suddenly 70's* (Greatest Hits of the 1970's)
- *The Best Smooth Jazz Ever!* (Disc I)
- *The Greatest Hits of All* (George Benson)

- *The Hits* (Faith Hill)
- *The Very Best of Kool and the Gang*
- *The Very Best of Chic*
- *The Very Best of the Bee Gees*
- *Tribute to Enya*

Additional CDs That Calm the Brain

- *The Most Relaxing Classical Album in the World*
- *The Most Relaxing Classical Album in the World—Ever!* (Disc 1)
- *The Most Relaxing New Age Music in the Universe*

WHO:	Elementary/Middle/High
WHEN:	After the lesson
CONTENT AREA(S):	All

- To assist students in recalling information following a lesson, have them walk, march, or dance around the room to high-energy, fast-paced music. Periodically, stop the music and have students form groups of three or four standing in close proximity. Have them recall a major concept covered in the lesson and discuss it with their respective groups. Then start the music again and have them walk in a different direction so that when they stop, they are not standing next to the same students. Have them repeat the procedure with another group and a second major concept.

WHO:	Elementary/Middle/High
WHEN:	Before a lesson
CONTENT AREA(S):	All

- Put your creative talents to work! Write an original song, rhyme, or rap to symbolize your understanding of a concept you have previously taught the class. Perform your creative effort for your students and teach it to them so that they can use the powerful effects of music to remember your content. They'll love you for it!

WHO:	Elementary/Middle/High
WHEN:	During a lesson
CONTENT AREA(S):	All

- To help students recognize the syllables in words, particularly the accented ones, have them stand by their desks, make a fist with their dominant hand, and push their arm straight out one time for every syllable in a multisyllabic word read aloud. If the syllable is an accented one, have students raise their arms toward the ceiling rather than straight out.

Adaptation: Have students clap out the syllables in a multisyllabic word.

WHO: Elementary/Middle/High
WHEN: After the lesson
CONTENT AREA(S):   All

• Have students work in cooperative groups to write a cinquain that symbolizes their understanding of a concept previously taught or content read. The format of a cinquain is as follows: first line—one word, second line—two words, third line—three words, fourth line—four words, last line—one word.

Example:

Brain

Social organism

Thinking, linking, connecting

Necessary for life itself

Life

WHO: Elementary/Middle/High
WHEN: After a lesson
CONTENT AREA(S):   All

• Following instruction in a major concept, have students write an original song, rhyme, or rap to symbolize their understanding of the concept previously taught. Students can be assigned this task for homework, if class time does not permit. Then on the following day, all students can attend the *Talent Show* where volunteers pretend to be on *American Idol* and get up and perform their original effort for the class. What a fun way to review content!

REFLECTION AND APPLICATION

How will I incorporate *music, rhythm, rhyme,* and *rap* into instruction to engage students' brains?

Standard/Objective: _____

_____

Activity: _____

_____

Standard/Objective: _____

_____

Activity: _____

_____

Standard/Objective: _____

_____

Activity: _____

_____

Standard/Objective: _____

_____

Activity: _____

_____

Standard/Objective: _____

_____

Activity: _____

_____

Standard/Objective: _____

_____

Activity: _____

_____

Strategy 12

Project-Based and Problem-Based Instruction

WHAT: DEFINING THE STRATEGY

Several years ago, I had the privilege of conducting a workshop in Scott County, Tennessee. As I was escorted to the campus of Scott County High School, I noticed a wood building on the grounds of the high school and asked about it. I was told that this was the Natural History Museum for the county. Because there was no such entity in the town, high school students, under the guidance of a visionary teacher took on the project of creating a museum that would be available to the entire county. I walked inside and quickly realized that this was project-based instruction and service learning in its best form. The museum was as well designed as any anywhere!

The project was interdisciplinary. Students had actually constructed the wood structure, researched to decide what parts of local history would be showcased in the museum. Then they integrated their writing skills by sending letters to people and agencies that could help them in securing the information they would need for the exhibits. Next, the art department got involved and designed what the museum, including the exhibits, would showcase. Finally, students were designated as *tour guides*. Working in cooperative groups, students wrote the scripts and prepared the oral presentations for the subsequent tours that would take local residents and visitors through the museum.

The museum is up and running and is a wonderful asset to the people of Scott County, Tennessee. It is such a service to the community as well as an unforgettable learning opportunity for students! I was so impressed that I took pictures, which I now include in some of my workshops as a prime example of the many benefits of project-based instruction.

WHY: THEORETICAL FRAMEWORK

Teaching problem-solving strategies using the interest of students of all disabilities and grade levels keeps them involved and capitalizes on their natural inclination to solve meaningful problems in the context of real life. (Algozzine, Campbell, & Wang, 2009b)

Engaging students physically builds problem-solving skills and assists learning because information is encapsulated for later recall. (Jensen, 2007)

A great deal can be achieved when the projects that teachers assign pull students into the learning by helping them make personal connections. (Karten, 2007)

When the learning is applicable to students' lives, students not only become more engaged but also they feel more responsible for finishing assignments and understand the relationship between their success in school and success in the real world. (Algozzine et al., 2009b)

Problem-based learning was shown to strongly affect a student's understanding of concepts and to moderately affect a student's ability to take the knowledge gleaned and apply it in new situations. (Gijbels, Dochy, Van den Bossche, & Segers, 2005)

Students need opportunities to interact within the larger context of solving real-world problems and conflicting situations. (Caine, Caine, McClintic, & Klimek, 2005)

Projects naturally organize students' attention because they begin with a purpose or a whole even though the parts eventually have to be addressed. (Caine et al., 2005)

When a new math skill is viewed within the context of a problem, English language learners have opportunities to develop language skills through discussion. (Coggins, Kravin, Coates, & Carrol, 2007)

When students interact with other students in a group while solving problems, both cognitive (basic) and metacognitive (higher-order) thinking skills are stimulated. (Posamentier & Jaye, 2006)

Project-based instruction provides the student with the intrinsic rewards of natural curiosity and a search for meaning. (Ronis, 2006)

Educators should use such authentic tools as projects, discussions, and portfolios in addition to paper-and-pencil tests to demonstrate students' comprehension of mathematics. (Ronis, 2006)

Students who think aloud when solving problems have more awareness of what information is needed to solve the problem and, therefore, think more systematically. (Posamentier & Jaye, 2006)

Movement strengthens the cerebellum, which is essential for efficient problem-solving skills and planning. (Feinstein, 2004)

When the student is problem solving or making decisions, parallel processing occurs in the brain. (Fogarty, 2001)

HOW: INSTRUCTIONAL ACTIVITIES

WHO:	Elementary/Middle/High
WHEN:	During a lesson
CONTENT AREA(S):	Mathematics

- Have students create their own math problems for other students to solve. When students enter the room, have one student's problem on the board for all students to solve as a *sponge activity*. The problem could provide a review of a problem-solving strategy already taught and could supply some needed practice. Students could earn extra points by solving one another's problems correctly either individually or with a partner.

WHO:	Elementary/Middle/High
WHEN:	During the lesson
CONTENT AREA(S):	All

- When introducing a new concept in class, create real-world problems incorporating the names of students in the class. Have students work individually, in pairs, or in small groups to solve the problems. For example, when teaching the concept of elapsed time, have a student in class, let's say her name is Denise, share her typical daily schedule, such as what time she gets up, gets to school, arrives home, eats dinner, goes to bed, and so forth. Write the schedule on the board. Then, have students figure out how much time elapses from the time Denise does one thing to the time she does something else. Using the context of a student's real-world experiences makes the content more relevant and meaningful.

WHO:	Elementary/Middle/High
WHEN:	During the lesson
CONTENT AREA(S):	All

- Identify multiple objectives from a number of content areas. Create a real-life project for students that will address all of the chosen objectives. For example, a project in which students write and produce a news program could address multiple objectives in a real-world, memorable context. Objectives for this project could include the following: researching major current or historical events to determine the stories to be included in the broadcast, writing news copy that is grammatically correct with a main idea sentence in each paragraph, or broadcasting the news using appropriate public speaking skills.

WHO:	Elementary/Middle/High
WHEN:	During the lesson
CONTENT AREA(S):	Mathematics

- Have students construct a class cookbook to apply their understanding of multiplying fractions. Have students find recipes for their favorite foods that have fractions of servings: for example, 2½ cups of flour, 2¼ cups of sugar, ¾ teaspoon of vanilla. Students then rewrite the recipe cutting it in half and then doubling and tripling it. Students can choose one version of the recipe to make as a project for homework.

WHO:	Elementary/Middle/High
WHEN:	After the lesson
CONTENT AREA(S):	Science

- To help them recall the parts of an animal cell, have students complete a project as a homework assignment. Have them make a pizza that displays their knowledge of the parts of the cell. Students will decide what toppings will be used to replicate parts of the cell such as pepperoni for the nucleus or for the cytoplasm. On a designated day, have students bring their pizzas to school and evaluate one another's pizzas based on a rubric they helped to develop. Following the evaluation, be sure the class eats their pizzas and enjoys a *Cellebration!*

WHO:	Elementary/Middle/High
WHEN:	After the lesson
CONTENT AREA(S):	History

- Following the study of a specific event in history, such as the Civil War, have students show what they have learned by creating a newspaper that will recount the major events during that time of history. Newspapers could include the following: a name, slogan, cost, index, front-page feature story, additional stories, advertisements, obituaries, crime stories, and so forth.

WHO:	Elementary/Middle/High
WHEN:	During the lesson
CONTENT AREA(S):	All

- Have students work in groups and follow these steps when solving math problems:
  - o Read the problem.
  - o Comprehend the problem.
  - o Analyze the problem.
  - o Plan an approach that can be used to solve the problem.
  - o Explore the approach to ascertain whether it will work.
  - o Use the plan to solve the problem.
  - o Verify the solution.
  - o Listen to and observe other students while solving the problem (Posamentier & Jaye, 2006).

  These steps could be put in a graphic organizer and placed as a visual on the wall for students to follow when solving math problems.

WHO:	Elementary/Middle/High
WHEN:	During the lesson
CONTENT AREA(S):	All

- Involve students in a project that will require that they collect and analyze data from a survey. Students should select a topic of interest to them and determine how they will collect the data, what the sample size should be, who should be sampled, and what type of graph (circle, line, bar, and the like) would be best for depicting the data. Topics could include some similar to the following: *What is your favorite brand of toothpaste? Should students in this school wear uniforms? What foods should be served in the cafeteria most often? What is your favorite subject and why?*

WHO:	Elementary/Middle/High
WHEN:	During the lesson
CONTENT AREA(S):	Mathematics

- Engage students in interdisciplinary cooperative learning projects such as the following. The class forms into student teams of four to six. Each team selects one football, basketball, or baseball team to follow for 10 to 20 games of the regular season. Each team will choose the most valuable player of the team for the 10- to 20-week period but must be ready to justify the choice using vital statistics as evidence. The team will plan and deliver a broadcast including a PowerPoint presentation during which they will report analysis and interpretation of the stats. They will also submit journals in which they have tracked the team's statistics.

WHO:	Elementary/Middle/High
WHEN:	After the lesson
CONTENT AREA(S):	Mathematics

- To assist students with the real-life skill of building a budget, have them work in cooperative groups. Give each group an allotted yearly income of, for example, $30,000. Have students plan a budget that allows for living expenditures such as housing, utilities, food, car note, gas for car, car and health insurance, and so forth. Have students research the average cost of each expenditure and build a realistic annual budget. This project goes a long way toward helping students realistically understand just how much money it actually takes to live.

WHO:	Elementary/Middle/High
WHEN:	During the lesson
CONTENT AREA(S):	All

- Place students in cooperative groups of four to six. Give each group a real-world problem to solve. Problems could include such topics as the following:
  - How would you increase parental participation in this school?
  - How would you decrease the unemployment rate in the country?
  - How can we increase the number of students taking advanced-placement classes in this school?

Have students collect and analyze data and work together to derive the best solution to the problem. Have each group write a paper outlining the problem and possible solution(s) and make an oral presentation to the class.

WHO: Elementary/Middle/High
WHEN: During the lesson
CONTENT AREA(S):   All

- When solving problems during class discussions, allow students to take turns sharing their ideas. Have them use sample sentence starters such as the following:
  - I realized that . . .
  - I agree with your thinking and would like to add . . .
  - I don't understand what you meant when you said . . .
  - I solved the problem this way . . .

WHO: Elementary/Middle/High
WHEN: During the lesson
CONTENT AREA(S):   All

- Engage students in a project in which they research how the content taught in school is used in real-world professions. For example, have them research how architects and engineers use math, scientists use science concepts, and so forth.

WHO: Elementary/Middle/High
WHEN: During the lesson
CONTENT AREA(S):   All

- Have students select an area of interest in which there is a real-world problem that needs to be addressed. Have students use the steps in the scientific process to investigate the problem and research possible solutions.

REFLECTION AND APPLICATION

> How will I incorporate *project-based* and *problem-based instruction* to engage students' brains?

Standard/Objective: _____

_____

Activity: _____

_____

Standard/Objective: _____

_____

Activity: _____

_____

Standard/Objective: _____

_____

Activity: _____

_____

Standard/Objective: _____

_____

Activity: _____

_____

Standard/Objective: _____

_____

Activity: _____

_____

Standard/Objective: _____

_____

Activity: _____

_____

Strategy 13

Reciprocal Teaching and Cooperative Learning

WHAT: DEFINING THE STRATEGY

Several years ago, I observed in a classroom where a teacher was providing answers for the calculus problems assigned for homework. He was at the front of the class working the problems on the board, in record time I might add. Not once did he ask a single question of a student to check for clarification. Not once did he ask what step should come next or what the answer should be. Not once did he ask students to teach one another how the answer was derived. By the time he finished, not only was every student confused but also so was I. I guess this teacher didn't read the research. Students learn 95% of what they teach to others.

When I was taught to teach more than 35 years ago, if two students were talking together about content, they were accused of cheating. If that is the case, I say, *"Let them cheat!"* Now, don't get me wrong. I'm not advocating being dishonest on tests. However, prior to testing, students benefit from discussing content with one another or from teaching one another what they are learning.

In the original definition of reciprocal teaching (Palinscar & Brown, 1984), the process was as follows. Students make predictions about a part of text to be read. Once the text is read, the group's discussion leader has the group discuss questions that have been raised. A group member then summarizes the content read thus far, and others clarify difficult concepts and make predictions about the following portion of text. Then the process continues. However, even periodically, stopping during class time and having students reteach what they are learning to a student sitting nearby is time well spent!

WHY: THEORETICAL FRAMEWORK

Cooperative group activities improve the learning for diverse students because they teach crucial social skills and reinforce concepts by allowing group members to discuss a variety of ideas. (Algozzine Campbell, & Wang, 2009b)

Because humans are social beings, working collaboratively elicits thinking that is superior to individual effort. (Costa, 2008)

It is natural for student conversations to get off the topic. Let them finish their personal discussion and then have them bring the conversation back around to the topic at hand. (Allen, 2008)

When individuals work together they are able to agree or disagree, state various perspectives, point out and settle differences, and examine alternatives. (Costa, 2008)

"Share what you know and feel memories grow". (Sprenger, 2007a)

Individual students' abilities can be nurtured when those students belong to a community of learners who engage in peer tutoring and working collaboratively to make sense of mathematics. (Posamentier & Jaye, 2006)

Children learn best when they have the opportunity to discuss ideas with their peers in a nose-to-nose and toes-to-toes interaction. (Gregory & Parry, 2006)

Without the metacognitive process of group debriefing following a cooperative activity, there is only minimal improvement in the group's ability to use a specific collaborative or social skill. (Gregory & Parry, 2006)

Diversity (mixing boys and girls and high and low achievers) within a cooperative group results in a better exchange of ideas. (Feinstein, 2004)

Students' memory is strengthened when they are provided with opportunities to teach the entire class, partners, or small groups. (Tileston, 2004)

Average and low achievers with or without learning disabilities showed greater achievement in classrooms where peer tutoring occurred than in those where it did not take place. (Posamentier & Jaye, 2006)

Cooperative learning enables teachers to access the positive, emotional brain of the learner. (Fogarty, 2001)

The three basic steps of reciprocal teaching include the following: (1) small group discussion, which enables students with lesser ability to achieve at higher levels; (2) independent group discussions, which help students take on the role of teacher while revising and making meaning of the content; and (3) scaffolding, which enables the teacher to provide support, when needed, and then, back away. (Coleman, Rivkin, & Brown, 1997)

> People remember 95% of what they are able to teach to someone else. (Glasser, 1990)
>
> People learn . . .
>
> 10% of what they read
>
> 20% of what they hear
>
> 30% of what they see
>
> 50% of what they both see and hear
>
> 70% of what they say as they talk
>
> 90% of what they say as they do a thing (Ekwall & Shanker, 1988, p. 370)

HOW: INSTRUCTIONAL ACTIVITIES

WHO: Elementary/Middle/High
WHEN: During the lesson
CONTENT AREA(S): All

• Have each student select a close partner (CP), a fellow student who sits so close in class that he or she can talk with this person, whenever necessary, and not have to get out of their seat. Stop periodically during a lesson and have students reteach a chunk of information just taught, brainstorm an idea, or review content prior to a test. Close partners can also reexplain a concept that might not be clear or easily understood by their partner.

WHO: Elementary/Middle/High
WHEN: During a lesson
CONTENT AREA(S): All

• Have students work together in cooperative groups, or *families,* of four to six students. They may be seated in groups already or taught to pick up their desks and arrange them into groups for a cooperative-learning activity and to put them back once the activity is over. It is recommended that the groups be of mixed ability levels or capitalize on the various multiple intelligences or talents of students.

Give each group the same task. Have them discuss the thought processes involved in completing the task and reach consensus as to the correct answer. Once the answer is agreed on, have each person in the group sign the paper that the answer is written on, verifying that they agree with the answer and, if called on randomly, could explain how the solution was derived to the entire class. This individual accountability helps to ensure that one person does not do all the work while other students watch their efforts.

WHO: Elementary/Middle/High
WHEN: During the lesson
CONTENT AREA(S): All

• When students have difficulty working together as a cooperative group, you may want to teach some social skills necessary for effective functioning. For example, construct a *T-chart* similar to the one here where each social skill is considered from two perspectives: (1) what it looks like and (2) what it sounds like. Social skills could include the following: paying undivided attention, encouraging one another, or critiquing ideas and not peers.

Encouraging

Looks Like	Sounds Like
Heads nodding	Way to go!
One person speaking	Good job!
Smiles	Good idea!
Eye contact	What do you think?

Observe each group and make a tally mark on a sheet each time the social skill is practiced by any student in the group. Provide feedback to the class during a debriefing following the cooperative activity. You may also assign a student in each group to fulfill the function of a *process observer* who collects the data for the group.

WHO: Elementary/Middle/High
WHEN: During the lesson
CONTENT AREA(S): All

• Another way to help ensure individual accountability is to assign group roles for students to fulfill during the cooperative learning activity. Some of the following roles can be assigned:
   o **Facilitator**—Ensures that the group stays on task and completes the assigned activity
   o **Scribe**—Writes down anything the group has to submit in writing
   o **Time Keeper**—Tells the group when half the time is over and when there is one minute remaining
   o **Reporter**—Gives an oral presentation to the class regarding the results of the group's work
   o **Materials Manager**—Collects any materials or other resources that the group needs to complete the task
   o **Process Observer**—Provides feedback to the group on how well they practiced their social skills during the cooperative learning activity

WHO:	Elementary/Middle/High
WHEN:	Before the lesson
CONTENT AREA(S):	All

- Have students draw the face of a clock. Have them write the numbers 12, 3, 6, and 9 in the appropriate places on the clock. Have students draw one line near each number. This clock becomes their vehicle for making appointments with their peers in class. Put on some fast-paced music and have students walk around the classroom and make appointments with four different students in class. They should write the name of the person they made each appointment with on the line next to the number so that later in the class, when it is time to meet with their appointment, they can remember with whom they made the appointment. See Chapter 10: Movement for a sample of the appointment clock.

  Stop periodically throughout the period or the day and have students keep their appointments. Appointments can be used to reteach a concept previously taught or to discuss an open-ended question pertaining to the lesson.

WHO:	Elementary/Middle/High
WHEN:	During the lesson
CONTENT AREA(S):	All

- For variety, have students make appointments, like those in the aforementioned activity, but have them use the cycle of the seasons of the year, rather than the face of the clock. The cycle is pictured in Chapter 10: Movement. Follow the same directions as those listed in the previous activity.

WHO:	Elementary/Middle/High
WHEN:	During the lesson
CONTENT AREA(S):	All

- One way to have students navigate through narrative or expository text is to have them engage in *partner reading*. Students could take turns participating in the *3-Ps* by reading a *page* or *paragraph* or *passing* their turn until the selection is complete. They could take turns quizzing their partners regarding what was just read.

WHO:	Elementary/Middle/High
WHEN:	During the lesson
CONTENT AREA(S):	All

- When students need to memorize facts in any content area, have them pair with a *drill partner*. Students work together to drill one another on the content (such as multiplication facts or content-area vocabulary definitions) for several minutes each day until both partners know and can recite the facts from memory. Give bonus points on the subsequent test if both partners score above a certain percentage or improve their score over a previous test.

WHO:	Elementary/Middle/High
WHEN:	During the lesson
CONTENT AREA(S):	All

• Have students use the *think, pair, share* technique. Students first individually *think* how they would respond to a question or solve a problem; then they *pair* with another student and *share* their thought processes and/or answer to the problem. Both students reach consensus as to the correct solution or answer. If their original answers differ, the discussion involved in convincing their partner that they are correct is invaluable to learning.

WHO:	Elementary/Middle/High
WHEN:	During the lesson
CONTENT AREA(S):	All

• Place students in cooperative groups. Have them participate in an activity called *jigsaw. Jigsaw's* name is derived from the fact that each student has only one piece of the puzzle, and it will take all students to make a whole. Each student in the cooperative group is accountable for teaching one section of a chapter. The procedure is as follows:

1. Give students time to prepare their part individually either in class or for homework.

2. Have them confer with a student in another group, who has the same part they do, to get and give ideas prior to teaching their original group.

3. Give each student a required number of minutes to teach their part to their original cooperative group. Individuals in each group start and stop teaching at the same time. If they finish before time is called, the student can quiz group members for understanding.

4. Conduct a whole class review that outlines the pertinent points that should have been made during each student's instruction. In this way, the entire class gets to hear the content at least twice, once from their partner and once from the teacher.

WHO:	Elementary/Middle/High
WHEN:	During the lesson
CONTENT AREA(S):	All

• While checking a homework or in-class assignment or brainstorming ideas, have students take their paper in hand and walk around the room to fast-paced music. Every time you stop the music, have each student pair with another student standing close by and *give* one answer to their partner and *get* one answer from their partner.

WHO: Elementary/Middle/High
WHEN: Before, during, or after the lesson
CONTENT AREA(S):   All

- When students are working with peers in small groups or talking to a partner, it is often difficult to get their attention. Create a signal and use it whenever you need students to pay attention to you. The signal can be a chime, a raised hand, a chant, a bell, or anything soothing that would not be abrasive to the brains of your students. Change the signal periodically because student brains appreciate novelty.

REFLECTION AND APPLICATION

> How will I incorporate *reciprocal teaching and cooperative learning* into instruction to engage students' brains?

Standard/Objective: _____

_____

Activity: _____

_____

Standard/Objective: _____

_____

Activity: _____

_____

Standard/Objective: _____

_____

Activity: _____

_____

Standard/Objective: _____

_____

Activity: _____

_____

Standard/Objective: _____

_____

Activity: _____

_____

Standard/Objective: _____

_____

Activity: _____

_____

Role Plays, Drama, Pantomimes, and Charades

WHAT: DEFINING THE STRATEGY

I go into classrooms when requested and teach model lessons where I take a teacher's objective and plan and teach a lesson to students while other teachers observe. The lesson always incorporates multiple strategies. One of my best lessons involved role play. I was asked to teach second-grade students to remember the nine planets (at that time Pluto was a planet). I began by asking students to visualize a time when they had looked in the sky at night. We discussed what they saw and that led into a discussion of what a planet actually is and which planet we occupy. Then I gave them the mnemonic device, *My very educated mother just served us nine pizzas,* to recall the planets in order from the sun. Of course, you know that the acrostic actually stands for **M**ercury, **V**enus, **E**arth, **M**ars, **J**upiter, **U**ranus, **N**eptune, and **P**luto.

The best part of the lesson was the next part—the role play. The entire class got up, and we pretended to be planets. He practiced revolving and rotating on our axis. I had made signs for the sun and for each of the planets, and I handed them out randomly to 10 students in the class. We then went outside, and I placed the sun in the middle and put the other students carrying signs in their orbits around the sun. You should have seen those students rotating and revolving while the sun stood still! We took turns so that each student in the class had an opportunity to be either the sun or a planet. Several days after the lesson, the teacher had the entire class write letters to tell me about how much they enjoyed the lesson and what they had learned. One of the letters will appear in a science book I am writing. The letters were so cute and full of pertinent information about the planets. You see, my lesson stuck to their brains. The role play not only reinforced the content but also made the lesson fun and more memorable.

WHY: THEORETICAL FRAMEWORK

When learning is physical, it is more motivating, engaging, and likely to be extended. (Jensen, 2008)

Whether the production is large or small, guiding students through a dramatic presentation can result in positive emotions and healthy learning for all involved. (Allen, 2008)

The brain-based learning strategies of role-play and simulations provide students with emotional connections to real life. (Karten, 2008)

In simulation or role-play contexts, learning is more enjoyable and meaningful, choice and creativity come into play, and pressure from negative evaluation is minimized. (Jensen, 2008)

Test scores for classes where students were involved in minidramas or vignettes were significantly higher than scores in three additional classes taught next door with traditional methods. (Allen, 2008)

Role play can be used to reinforce learning in a mathematics class. Examples would include having students make change or take measurements. (Sprenger, 2007a)

Role plays are most effective when illustrating key events, demonstrating critical roles of historical figures, and showing the process of concepts that come in sequential order. (Udvari-Solner & Kluth, 2008)

Role play motivates students to participate, enhances enthusiasm and recall of information, and stores the information in the body as well as the brain. (Jensen, 2007)

As students involve their bodies in the comprehension of concepts and ideas through role plays and skits, they are able to understand the material in a new way. (Sprenger, 2007a)

Although students can find role plays or enactments very engaging, they can take a great deal of time and are not as effective if the teacher does not have students explain the important concepts enacted. (Marzano, 2007)

Role plays use visual, spatial, linguistic, and bodily modalities, and, therefore, not only access students' emotions but also enable students to comprehend at much deeper levels than a lecture would. (Gregory & Parry, 2006)

It can be a very engaging and highly effective activity to have a group of students act out or role play a word problem. (Bender, 2005)

Role play and pretend play enable children to experience empathy and determine what course of action is necessary in any given social situation. (McCormick Tribune Foundation, 2004)

Simulations increase meaning, facilitate the transfer of knowledge, and are highly motivating. (Wolfe, 2001)

HOW: INSTRUCTIONAL ACTIVITIES

WHO:	Elementary/Middle/High
WHEN:	During the lesson
CONTENT AREA(S):	All

• Have students *body spell* the letters of their content-area vocabulary words. First, have them visualize the word. Then have them move their bodies according to the placement of the letters in the word. For example, let's suppose the word we need to spell is "play." The lowercase *p* in play falls below the line so to body spell it, the student should bend toward the floor from the waist with the arms extended as if to touch the toes. The *l* in play extends above the line so to body spell it, students should put both arms up and reach for the sky. The *a* in play falls on the line, so the student should put both arms out to the side. Finally, the *y* in play falls below the line (just like the *p*) so the arms are once again positioned to touch the toes. The student then puts it all together and spells the entire word, *play*. They say each letter of the word as they *body spell* it. Once students learn the technique, they can spell any word. Have them spell content-area vocabulary such as Mississippi or photosynthesis. As students become more confident with their body spelling, they enjoy spelling words faster and faster, and because the words are being placed in procedural memory, the spelling grades automatically improve.

WHO:	Elementary
WHEN:	After the lesson
CONTENT AREA(S):	Mathematics

• Have students take turns running the classroom store where items are bought and sold. Place items in the store that sell for the increments of money previously studied, such as a penny, nickel, dime, quarter, and dollar. Place play money in the store and have students take turns buying and selling the items. Students can practice the skills of counting, determining the coins necessary to purchase specific items, making change, and so forth.

WHO:	Elementary/Middle/High
WHEN:	During the lesson
CONTENT AREA:	Mathematics

• To more clearly understand the steps in a multistep word problem, have students take turns getting up and acting out each step of the word problem. This role play will work with a large majority of math problems and can go a long way in helping students who need a visual depiction of the problem.

WHO:	Elementary/Middle/High
WHEN:	During the lesson
CONTENT AREA:	History

- Following a lesson on a major historical event such as the first Thanksgiving or the signing of the Declaration of Independence, have students create a dramatic presentation of the event, incorporating major characters and details in sequential order.

WHO:	Elementary
WHEN:	During the lesson
CONTENT AREA(S):	Science

- Have students demonstrate an understanding of the rotation and revolution of the planets by dividing them into groups of ten. One student in each group pretends to be the sun and the other nine revolve around the sun in order from closest to the sun to farthest from the sun while simultaneously rotating on their axis. Give students signs to hold up for the planets that they represent so that other students have a visual.

WHO:	Elementary/Middle/High
WHEN:	During the lesson
CONTENT AREA(S):	Language arts

- Have students participate in *Reader's Theater* by dramatizing a story previously read. Assign parts to members of the class and have them act out their respective parts. This role play goes a long way toward improving comprehension of narrative text.

WHO:	Elementary/Middle/High
WHEN:	During the lesson
CONTENT AREA(S):	Mathematics

- Teach geometric terms ensuring that students understand their meanings, terms such as *line, line segment, ray, right angle, obtuse angle,* and *acute angle.* Show students an action for each definition. Then have students stand up beside their desks and role-play the definitions that you just demonstrated. For example, to demonstrate the term *line*, have students point both arms out to their sides and point their fingers to indicate that a line has no end points. To demonstrate *line segment*, have them point their arms straight out but ball their fingers into fists to demonstrate that a line segment has two end points. Have them demonstrate a *ray* by pointing the arms out and making the left fingers into a fist while pointing the right fingers out straight because the ray only has one end point.

Students can role play angles by extending both arms to simulate right, obtuse, and acute angles. Involve students in a game by having them use their arms to make the terms as you randomly say the terms. This game is a lot of fun while putting the terms into procedural or muscle memory.

WHO:	Elementary/Middle/High
WHEN:	After the lesson
CONTENT AREA(S):	All

- Have students work in cooperative groups to prepare a television news broadcast related to a concept previously taught in class. By the time students complete this interdisciplinary project, they will have written a copy for the news broadcast summarizing the math concept taught, decided which visuals or graphics they need in the broadcast (including a PowerPoint presentation, if necessary), and selected a member of the group to deliver the broadcast on air. The class will use a rubric that they helped develop to vote on the most effective presentation.

WHO:	Elementary/Middle/High
WHEN:	After the lesson
CONTENT AREA(S):	All

- Review vocabulary by playing *Charades*. Write the words on separate 3-inch × 5-inch index cards. Have students take turns coming to the front of the room, selecting a card at random, and acting out or role-playing the definition of the selected word. The student cannot speak but must use only gestures to get their classmates to name the word. The first student to guess which vocabulary word is being acted out wins a point for guessing the word. The student with the most points at the culmination of the game is the winner.

WHO:	Elementary/Middle/High
WHEN:	During the lesson
CONTENT AREA(S):	Science

- Following a discussion of the properties of states of matter, have students pretend to be molecules. Divide the class into three groups. Have one group role-play as if they are solids by standing rigidly packed together; another group pretends to be liquids by moving around one another but not apart; and a third group role plays molecules in gases by moving almost independent of one another and far apart. Those students in your class who exhibit characteristics of ADHD should be placed in the third group so that they can bounce around the room for a few seconds.

WHO:	Middle/High
WHEN:	During the lesson
CONTENT AREA(S):	English/history

- Following a discussion of the judicial system, have students establish a peer court in which they try a character in a novel or a historical figure for a predetermined offense. Roles of the judge, bailiff, jury, witnesses, prosecuting attorney, and defense attorney are assigned and carried out by members of the class.

WHO: Elementary/Middle/High
WHEN: After the lesson
CONTENT AREA(S):   All

- Have students take turns role-playing that they are you, the teacher. Have them volunteer to come to the front of the room and pretend, as the teacher, to reteach the lesson previously taught. Give each student a maximum of three minutes. This activity will give you an idea of which concepts have been understood by your students and which need reteaching. Remember that you learn what you teach and that most brains need to hear something a minimum of three times before the information actually sticks. As a side benefit, you will get to see your teaching through your students' eyes.

REFLECTION AND APPLICATION

How will I incorporate *role plays* into instruction to engage students' brains?

Standard/Objective: _____
_____.

Activity: _____
_____.

Standard/Objective: _____
_____.

Activity: _____
_____.

Standard/Objective: _____
_____.

Activity: _____
_____.

Standard/Objective: _____
_____.

Activity: _____
_____.

Standard/Objective: _____
_____.

Activity: _____
_____.

Standard/Objective: _____
_____.

Activity: _____
_____.

Strategy 15

Storytelling

WHAT: DEFINING THE STRATEGY

Tell your students the following story to teach the continents. It will take you less than one minute.

There once was a man named **North**. His last name was **America.**

He fell in love with a beautiful woman named **South**. They got married and she took his name so she became **South America**. They honeymooned in **Europe**. This couple was blessed to have four daughters whose names all began with the letter A. Their names were **Africa**, **Antarctica**, **Asia**, and **Australia**.

The End

By the time you have told this story aloud at least three times and students have gotten up and told the story to several partners in the room, students remember the continents. Why? Because the continents are not learned in isolation. They are learned within the context of a story. Stories not only allow students' brains to relax but also they help them have an easier time of retaining the newly acquired material (Jensen, 2000).

If you don't think stories are important to all brains, watch when a speaker or minister tells a story. Everyone gets quiet! However, I don't believe in telling stories to waste students' time. Every time you tell a story, be sure that it teaches a concept. When students remember the story, they remember the point you were trying to make.

WHY: THEORETICAL FRAMEWORK

Because stories can include important points, various types of content can be encoded in them. (Allen, 2008)

Concrete images in stories activate our emotions and sense of meaning and supply cues and contexts for new information. (Markowitz & Jensen, 2007)

It may be easier for students to work in groups of three as they begin to create make-believe stories that include facts and people to be remembered. (Caine, Caine, McClintic, & Klimek, 2005)

Students often remember stories better when they create original ones. (Allen, 2008)

Children naturally develop a sense of story and the brain's fascination with story continues throughout our lives. (Caine et al., 2005)

A story, a dramatic representation of the content, does not require a great deal of preparation when it is in its simplest form. (Marzano, 2003)

After a period of intense learning, storytelling enables the brain to relax and facilitates the retention of newly acquired material. (Jensen, 2000)

Stories, or narratives, can be powerful for storing curriculum content because they connect to one's personal life, are integrated, and held together by a structure that is familiar. (Nuthall, 1999)

The conflict or plot of a story can be addressed through emotional memory. (Sprenger, 1999)

Story problems in which real objects are distributed in equal shares help prekindergarten through Grade 2 students understand the concepts of division and multiplication. (National Council of Teachers of Mathematics, 2000)

Students' ability to listen and reason is improved during storytelling because they use the auditory modality with the frontal lobes of the brain to follow the story's plot. (Storm, 1999)

HOW: INSTRUCTIONAL ACTIVITIES

WHO: Elementary/Middle/High
WHEN: During the lesson
CONTENT AREA(S):   Language arts

• Create stories, fictional or fact, that can be used to illustrate a concept that you are teaching. Integrate the stories into your lesson delivery and watch students more easily retain the concept. If your story is humorous or emotional, the recall value is enhanced.

WHO:	Elementary/Middle/High
WHEN:	During the lesson
CONTENT AREA(S):	All

• Have students create stories, fictional or fact, which can be used to remember a concept that has been taught. Stories are particularly helpful when recalling a multistep process or events that happen in sequential order. Have students retell their stories several times to their classmates. Have them recall their original stories each time they attempt to remember the key concept on which the story is based.

WHO:	Elementary/Middle
WHEN:	During the lesson
CONTENT AREA(S):	Mathematics

• Read aloud to the class any of the appropriate books in the bibliography, *Have You Read Any Math Lately?* found on page 147 of *Mathematics Worksheets Don't Grow Dendrites: 20 Numeracy Strategies that Engage the Brain* (2009). These books include *Skittles Riddles Math* by Barbara McGrath or *How Big Is a Foot?* by Rolf Myller. The first time you read the books aloud, do so for the enjoyment of the literature. Then revisit the book at another time and select a math skill or strategy from the story. The context of the story will help students remember the skill being taught.

WHO:	Elementary/Middle/High
WHEN:	During the lesson
CONTENT AREA(S):	Language arts

• Select literary works that contain numerous examples of language arts skills and strategies from the curriculum to be taught. Although a few titles are listed below as examples, any story or poem that contains examples of the skill can be used. Read the story or poem aloud to the class initially for enjoyment. Reread parts of the story on a subsequent day pointing out examples of the skill or strategy to be taught. Have students look for examples in this or other literary works.

Literature Used to Teach Skills and Strategies

Main Idea and Details

The Important Book by Margaret Wise Brown

Cause and Effect

The Day Jimmy's Boa Ate the Wash by Trinka Hayes Noble

Sequence of Events

Thomas' Snowsuit by Robert Munsch

Point of View

    The Pain and the Great One by Judy Blume

    Encounter (story of Christopher Columbus from the Native's point of view) by Jane Yolen

    My Brothers' Flying Machine (story of the Wright Brothers from the sister's point of view) by Jane Yolen

Parts of Speech/Figurative Language

    The King Who Rained by Fred Gwynne

    A Chocolate Moose for Dinner by Fred Gwynne

    The Parts of Speech Series by Brian Cleary

    The Parts of Speech Series by Ruth Heller

WHO:	Elementary/Middle/High
WHEN:	During the lesson
CONTENT AREA(S):	All

- Following a read aloud or the silent reading of a story or content-area unit of study, have students retell the story to a partner with story events in the correct sequential order.

WHO:	Elementary/Middle/High
WHEN:	During the lesson
CONTENT AREA(S):	Language arts

- Have students work individually or in cooperative groups to use the *narrative chaining* method by creating an original story linking together unrelated terms, concepts, or words in a list.

WHO:	Elementary/Middle/High
WHEN:	Before the lesson
CONTENT AREA(S):	All

- Consult the text *Math and Children's Literature*, which provides numerous examples of stories that can be used to teach various math principles. Refer to the index of the *Math and Children's Literature* book to find children's books that will teach or reinforce a concept being taught.

WHO:	Middle/High
WHEN:	During the lesson
CONTENT AREA(S):	Mathematics

- Tell students *The Story of the Algebraic Equation* to help them understand one step in solving equations. This story also incorporates the strategies of movement, role play, and metaphor. Seven students hold cards that represent the numbers and signs in the algebraic equation *3y + 10 = 2y + 18*. *3y* and *2y* should be female students. *Ten* and *18* should be male students. The cards for *10* and *2y* should have *−10* and *−2y*, respectively, written on the backs. Students role-play the story as it is read.

The Story of the Algebraic Equation

3y + 10 = 2y + 18

Once upon a time, there were two families that lived on either side of a busy street called *equal street*. Each family had two children (one teenage daughter and one younger son). One day the teenage daughters, 3y and 2y, made a date to go to the mall. However, there was a problem. Each daughter had been asked to babysit a younger brother. 3y had to babysit 10 and 2y had to babysit 18.

The girls desperately wanted to get together to go to the mall. Therefore, daughter 3y suggested that she send her younger brother 10 to cross equal street so that he could play with her friend's brother, 18. Now, there was one peculiar thing about this particular town. Whenever anyone crossed equal street, they had to turn around and cross it backward. So younger brother 10 turned backward and crossed the street. The two boys were very happy because now they could play together.

There was only one problem. To be all alone with no one to bother them, the boys had to get rid of big sister 2y. That was all right with big sister 2y because she wanted to go to the mall with her friend 3y anyway. So she said good-bye to her brother and crossed equal street, backward of course, and she and her friend 3y could be all alone to proceed to the mall. The girls had a wonderful time and so did the boys.

When the girls returned from the mall, they were in a world of trouble because their parents had told them over and over again never to leave their younger brothers unattended. But you know as well as I do that for generations older sisters have left younger brothers unattended. That's just the way the story goes!

REFLECTION AND APPLICATION

How will I incorporate *storytelling* into instruction to engage my students' brains?

Standard/Objective: _____

_____

Activity: _____

_____

Standard/Objective: _____

_____

Activity: _____

_____

Standard/Objective: _____

_____

Activity: _____

_____

Standard/Objective: _____

_____

Activity: _____

_____

Standard/Objective: _____

_____

Activity: _____

_____

Standard/Objective: _____

_____

Activity: _____

_____

Standard/Objective: _____

_____

Activity: _____

_____

Strategy 16

Technology

WHAT: DEFINING THE STRATEGY

I recently saw an announcement in a university catalog for a new course being offered titled *interpersonal communication*. In small type, underneath the title were the following words: *This class will be taught online.* I don't know about you but, to me, that seems like an oxymoron.

Technological advances have revolutionized all aspects of our lives including how educators teach and students learn. We have progressed from blackboards to SMART boards and from paper and pencil to graphing calculators. More than 15 years ago, the SCANS Report (Secretary's Commission on Achieving Necessary Skills, 1991) lists technology as one of the eight major competencies essential for success in the real world of work. It is even a truer statement today. To prepare students for future success, visualize the following classroom facilitated by a technologically knowledgeable teacher. In one corner of the classroom, a group of students is developing a PowerPoint presentation as a culminating activity to a chapter on the American Revolution. Several other students are on the Internet locating information for a project in which they are creating a Web page for their class. Another group is creating a role play, which they will video and post to YouTube. While yet another group is watching a distance learning telecast of a science experiment, which they will perform for the class next week.

Technology is crucial. However, the longer I work with students the more convinced I am that the strategy of technology is only one of 20 and should be balanced with the other 19. All the strategies help to foster the interpersonal skills that are essential for meaningful personal and professional relationships in the real world. Too many students are so caught up in text messaging and e-mailing others that they have lost the art of true interpersonal communication.

WHY: THEORETICAL FRAMEWORK

Students of all ability levels can use technology "to process, demonstrate, and retain and share information and communication." (Karten, 2009, p. 196)

Assistive technology can support the participation of students with disabilities in whole class and small group discussion. (Udvari-Solner & Kluth, 2008)

Literacy in the digital age refers not only to writing and reading but also to a student's ability to use technology when analyzing the volume of information that exists. (Sheffield, 2007)

A number of students who are failing traditional classroom courses are able to avail themselves of technology-based courses in an effort to catch up with their peers. (Barr & Parrett, 2007)

Higher achievement and greater understanding in math is achieved when technology is used for nonroutine applications and not for routine calculations. (Sousa, 2007)

Self-paced, interactive, Internet-based K–12 courses enable students to work full- or part-time while simultaneously pursuing their education. (Barr & Parrett, 2007)

When the inquiry-based learning model is paired with dynamic geometric software programs, students are able to discover relationships, make hypotheses, and defend assumptions. (Posamentier & Jaye, 2006)

Technology is not the lesson itself but a tool for teaching the lesson. (Hiraoka, 2006)

When calculators are used to explore and problem solve in math, students' view them as tools that can only enhance the learning. (Guerrero, Walker, & Dugdale, 2004)

The International Society of Technology lists the following skills as essential for all students to have: knowledge of databases, word processing, CD-ROM searches, e-library use, online maps, spreadsheets, Internet searches, desktop publishing, presentation and hypermedia software, and e-mail. (Barr & Parrett, 2007)

Interactive technology (such as computer animation or HyperStudio) makes the learning fun and exciting for adolescents. (Feinstein, 2004)

Technology can assist all students in developing number sense but is particularly helpful for students with special needs. (National Council of Teachers of Mathematics, 2000)

HOW: INSTRUCTIONAL ACTIVITIES

WHO: Elementary/Middle/High
WHEN: During a lesson
CONTENT AREA(S):   All

• Involve students in content with the use of a SMART or Promethean board. These technological presentation devices enable the teacher to access the Internet and display it to the entire class as well as show the class other computer programs of interest. The SMART board can also be used to display regular writing when done with the special markers provided.

WHO: Elementary/Middle/High
WHEN: During or after a lesson
CONTENT AREA(S):   All

• Use a piece of technology called a document camera (often referred to as an ELMO) to provide visuals for students. The camera must be connected to an LCD projector and serves a similar function to the old opaque projector, which is now extinct. Anything placed underneath the camera will provide a visual for the class. Therefore, you can use the camera to write notes, work math problems, or show student work to the class. Even if you read a story to the class from a picture book, the pictures will show to the entire class. The document camera can also be connected to a computer for easy toggle back and forth for showing videos or Internet connections.

WHO: Elementary/Middle/High
WHEN: During or after a lesson
CONTENT AREA(S):   All

• Teach or review the basic functions of a word processing program such as Word and have students produce a paper on a content-related topic using that program.

WHO: Elementary/Middle/High
WHEN: During or after a lesson
CONTENT AREA(S):   Mathematics

• During a math lesson, have students use the technology of a TI-73 or TI-83/84 plus graphing calculator to solve equations.

WHO: Elementary/Middle/High
WHEN: During a lesson
CONTENT AREA(S):   All

• Have students search the Internet for jobs in the real world that require the content knowledge being learned in school. Because the purpose of the brain is to survive in the real world, students often ask teachers why they have to learn a specific skill or concept and what that concept has to do with their survival in the real world. By engaging students in this conversation, that question might not have to be asked.

WHO: Elementary/Middle/High
WHEN: During a lesson
CONTENT AREA(S):   All

• Engage students in a project or problem where they need to display their knowledge of Excel to create charts or graphs.

WHO: Elementary/Middle/High
WHEN: During a lesson
CONTENT AREA(S):   All

• Have students work in cooperative groups to produce a PowerPoint presentation related to course content to be remembered. The presentation will be shown to and evaluated by classmates.

WHO: Elementary/Middle/High
WHEN: After a lesson
CONTENT AREA(S):   All

• Require students to complete a research report related to an assigned topic. At least, three of the references must come from Web sites accessed on the Internet. The sites must be appropriately listed in the bibliography of the report and incorporate information pertinent to the body of the paper.

WHO: Middle/High
WHEN: After a lesson
CONTENT AREA(S):   All

• Have students create an original song, rhyme, or a rap, as suggested in Chapter 11: Music to demonstrate their understanding of course content. Select the best creative efforts and have those students follow the necessary directions to post their songs, rhymes, or raps on iTunes for others to enjoy.

WHO: Middle/High
WHEN: After a lesson
CONTENT AREA(S):   All

• After students create an original song, rhyme, or rap, as suggested in Chapter 11: Music, or create a visual such as the original commercial in Chapter 19: Work Study, have them post their creative effort on YouTube.

WHO: Elementary/Middle/High
WHEN: After a lesson
CONTENT AREA(S):   Language arts

   • Have students apply the characteristics of letter writing by assigning them to correspond with a pen pal in another part of the world via e-mail. Each e-mail sent should adhere to an appropriate form and demonstrate the correct use of grammar.

WHO: Elementary/Middle/High
WHEN: After a lesson
CONTENT AREA(S):   All

   • Have students view a distance-learning telecast with appropriate follow-up activities that reinforce content being taught.

REFLECTION AND APPLICATION

How will I incorporate *technology* into instruction to engage students' brains?

Standard/Objective: _____

_____

Activity: _____

_____

Standard/Objective: _____

_____

Activity: _____

_____

Standard/Objective: _____

_____

Activity: _____

_____

Standard/Objective: _____

_____

Activity: _____

_____

Standard/Objective: _____

_____

Activity: _____

_____

Standard/Objective: _____

_____

Activity: _____

_____

Standard/Objective: _____

_____

Activity: _____

_____

Strategy **17**

Visualization and Guided Imagery

WHAT: DEFINING THE STRATEGY

In his book *The Seven Habits of Highly Effective People*, Stephen Covey (1996) relates that everything happens twice, once in the mind, and once in reality. Because I am a trainer for that program, I took his words to heart. I saw myself writing my first book in my mind before I ever turned on the computer to write a single word. I envisioned the introduction, which chapters would be included, what each chapter would contain, and how I would end it. I really saw the book as meeting a need for teachers and administrators because it would be the first time that many, if not all, of the brain-compatible strategies for delivering instruction would be in one text. Evidently, I was correct in my assumption. At this revision, the book is in its 12th printing and has sold more copies than I ever could visualize.

The strategy of visualization also works for teachers and students. Teachers should visualize every one of their students experiencing success every year. This is the first step toward ensuring that it happens!

Visualize when you were young and you went outside and played. Remember that you saw yourself as something else and your friend as another character. The tree in your yard was not a tree, but your house. In other words, you imagined. One reason that some of today's students have a difficult time comprehending what they read is because in this world of vivid visuals found on computer screens and in video games, students have had little opportunity to use their imaginations. And yet if there are no pictures in a novel, good readers have to visualize the action in the story. Otherwise, there is little or no comprehension. This strategy provides opportunities for students to use their imaginations to facilitate understanding across the curriculum. Continue reading this chapter and find out how.

WHY: THEORETICAL FRAMEWORK

Practicing visualization can help the brain access important information and preexpose it to meaningful data. (Jensen, 2008)

"A picture in your mind creates a memory you can find." (Sprenger, 2007)

Coaches have been aware for a long time that when athletes mentally rehearse their performance, they perform better than when they do not use imagery. (Sousa, 2006)

Like great athletes (i.e., skiers and golfers) and actors, students can visualize a performance before it happens. (Caine, Caine, McClintic, & Klimek, 2005)

Visualization enhances learning and retention of information because, during mental imagery, the same sections of the brain's visual cortex are activated than when the eyes are actually processing input from the real world. (Sousa, 2006)

A meta-analysis of 1,500 students representing nine separate studies showed that those who visualized or used more mental imagery while learning engaged in creativity during discussions, modeling, and assessments. (LeBoutillier & Marks, 2003)

Two to three minutes of quiet time along with music and visualization techniques can be used in class to help students relax their brains. (Fogarty, 2001)

In a study at Oxford University, one group of elementary students was asked to visualize prior to testing, whereas a second group simply took the test. The group that visualized prior to testing scored higher. (Drake, 1996)

The image is the greatest instrument of instruction. If the majority of classroom time was spent ensuring that students are forming proper images, the instructor's work would be indefinitely facilitated. (Dewey, 1938)

HOW: INSTRUCTIONAL ACTIVITIES

WHO: Elementary/Middle/High
WHEN: Before the lesson
CONTENT AREA(S):   All

• To increase the confidence of your students, have them visualize themselves being successful in your class. Have them picture themselves participating in class, scoring high on tests, and making a great grade at the culmination of the quarter, semester, or year. Ask students where they see themselves in one, five, or ten years. If the images are negative, do everything you can to change that picture. Remember, *everything happens twice, once in the mind and once in reality* (Covey, 1996)!

WHO:	Elementary/Middle/High
WHEN:	During the lesson
CONTENT AREA(S):	Mathematics

• To provide practice in visualizing, as you read a word problem aloud, have students imagine each step of the problem. Have them see in their mind what is happening and then determine what operations are needed to solve the problem. Stop periodically and have students draw what they are visualizing.

WHO:	Elementary/Middle/High
WHEN:	During the lesson
CONTENT AREA(S):	All

• Read aloud to students at all grade levels for purposes of information, enjoyment, or to teach a skill or strategy. As you read, have students visualize what is happening. Stop periodically and have students describe the scenes in their minds to one another, and then compare them to the original text.

WHO:	Elementary/Middle/High
WHEN:	During the lesson
CONTENT AREA(S):	All

• As students read a novel or content-area passage independently, teach them how to visualize the scenes or events using each of their senses. Have them answer the following question: What do you see, hear, feel, touch, and taste as you visualize the passage you are reading?

WHO:	Elementary/Middle/High
WHEN:	During the lesson
CONTENT AREA(S):	All

• Have students work individually or in groups to create visual images that link a word to its definition. The more absurd the visual image, the easier it is for the brain to remember the definition. For example, to remember the definition of the *hippocampus,* a part of the brain that determines what information will eventually get into long-term memory, have students visualize a herd of hippopotamus walking on a college campus through a gate. This image depicts the *hippocampus* as the *gateway to long-term memory.*

WHO:	Elementary/Middle/High
WHEN:	During the lesson
CONTENT AREA(S):	Mathematics

• Have students visualize what a given shape would look like rotated 180 degrees, flipped vertically, or turned 90 degrees. Have them describe or draw the resulting figure.

WHO:	Elementary/Middle/High
WHEN:	During the lesson
CONTENT AREA(S):	Science

- Have students read through the sequence of steps in a lab they are getting ready to complete. Then have them visualize each step. You may want them to provide an illustration for several of the steps to facilitate their understanding of the laboratory procedures (Ogle, 2000).

WHO:	Elementary/Middle/High
WHEN:	During the lesson
CONTENT AREA(S):	Science

- As you use guided imagery to orally describe a bodily function, have students visualize themselves involved in the process such as a red blood cell coursing through the body or a piece of food involved in the process of digestion. As a red blood cell, have them imagine the salty taste, the warm temperature, or the wetness that they would experience.

WHO:	Elementary/Middle/High
WHEN:	During the lesson
CONTENT AREA(S):	Physical education

- To improve the quality of their physical performance, have students visualize themselves being successful, such as getting the base hit, making the basket, completing the pass, or jumping the farthest. These positive images help to increase confidence in the brain and improve physical prowess.

WHO:	Elementary/Middle/High
WHEN:	During the lesson
CONTENT AREA(S):	History

- Have students mentally transport themselves into a specific period of history being studied, such as the Civil War or the French Revolution and visualize themselves in that period. Have them ask and answer the following questions: What do you see? How are you dressed? What's going on around you? These images will help to make history more relevant and memorable.

WHO:	Elementary/Middle/High
WHEN:	During the lesson
CONTENT AREA(S):	All

- Show students a content-area visual such as a math formula, vocabulary word, or science process. After a period of time, remove the visual and ask them to visualize the concept and write it from memory. Repeat the process several times because the brain needs repetition.

WHO: Elementary/Middle/High
WHEN: Before the lesson
CONTENT AREA(S):   All

• To alleviate anxiety prior to any test, have students take deep breaths and visualize themselves successfully completing each item on the test. This activity, in addition to well-taught lessons incorporating the brain-compatible strategies, gives students the confidence they need to do well!

REFLECTION AND APPLICATION

How will I incorporate *visualization* into instruction to engage students' brains?

Standard/Objective: _____

_____.

Activity: _____

_____.

Standard/Objective: _____

_____.

Activity: _____

_____.

Standard/Objective: _____

_____.

Activity: _____

_____.

Standard/Objective: _____

_____.

Activity: _____

_____.

Standard/Objective: _____

_____.

Activity: _____

_____.

Standard/Objective: _____

_____.

Activity: _____

_____.

Strategy 18

Visuals

WHAT: DEFINING THE STRATEGY

Have you flown in an airplane recently? If so, you will remember that it is not sufficient for the flight attendants to simply *tell* you what to do with your seat belt and the other myriad instructions they need to give. They have to show you. They either get out in the aisle and demonstrate while holding the apparatus or show you what to do via a video. Why? Even airline personnel know that merely telling human beings what they need to know is probably the least effective form of getting the information across to them. Brains need a visual to accompany the information. I fly so frequently that not only have I memorized the dialogue of what to do but also I can actually physically show you where the exits are. If you ever attend one of my workshops, I will be more than happy to demonstrate this crucial information for you (smile).

The Chinese knew this fact thousands of years ago when they created the following proverb:

> *Tell me, I forget*
>
> *Show me, I remember.*
>
> *Involve me, I understand!*

There is even physical evidence to support that the visual cortex in the brains of students today is actually physically thicker than it was in my brain when I was their age. Look at all of the information that today's students are taking in visually. They play video games; they spend hours on the computer; they watch television. These activities would make the visual modality a strong one for many of your students. That is why you need the strategy of visuals.

WHY: THEORETICAL FRAMEWORK

Thinking with visuals (murals, drawings, computer graphics, paintings) is an effective tool for elaboration because words and pictures can show great detail. (Jensen, 2009b)

Visual aids provide students with a point of focus and improve learning as students encounter the following stages of acquiring new concepts: acquisition, proficiency, maintenance, and generalization. (Algozzine, Campbell, & Wang, 2009b)

Visuals can often help to communicate a teacher's message in a more powerful way than words because visuals can be taken in quickly and remembered by the brain. (Allen, 2008)

Because the eyes can take in 30 million bits of information per second, teachers should provide images and moving pictures when instructing students. (Jensen, 2007)

Concept maps, flowcharts, graphic icons, cartoons, sketches, and drawings are all visuals that help students understand and process new content. (Allen, 2008)

"Visual learners take in the world through pictures and words and need to see the teacher solve a problem first to understand it." (Sprenger, 2007a)

For English learners, visual tools in math offer visual ways of thinking about relationships and communicating information. (Coggins, Kravin, Coates, & Carrol, 2007)

After about two weeks, the effects of direct instruction diminish on the brains of students, but the effects of visuals and those images taken in peripherally continue to increase during the same period of time. (Jensen, 2007)

When visuals and the auditory information used to explain those visuals go together, they can be helpful. Otherwise, pictures can interfere with a person's ability to listen to the words. (Posamentier & Jaye, 2006)

"Visual learners take in the world through words and through pictures." (Sprenger, 2007a)

Even though rote learning plays some part, students in Singapore comprehend abstract concepts by using visual tools. (Prystay, 2004)

According to Madeline Hunter, teachers can use both static and emerging visuals. Emerging visuals are those that appear as the lesson is taught, such as teacher and students creating graphic organizers together or using a SMART board. Static visuals are those that have been previously prepared such as charts, photos, and graphics. (Hunter, 2004)

Because peripheral vision enables one to see beyond the selected focal point, teachers should be mindful of the visuals in the learning situation. (Fogarty, 2001)

HOW: INSTRUCTIONAL ACTIVITIES

WHO: Elementary/Middle/High
WHEN: During the lesson
CONTENT AREA(S):   All

• Facilitate lecture or discussion with visuals by writing key words and phrases or drawing pictures on a dry erase, SMART board, or document camera. For example, write the *noun* and the words "person," "place," "thing," and "idea" as you explain its definition or draw and label a picture of the heart as you explain its function. Color leaves its imprint on the brain. Write with a blue marker, which works well for most students' brains. Emphasize keys words or phrases in red.

WHO: Elementary/Middle/High
WHEN: During the lesson
CONTENT AREA(S):   All

• As you deliver a lecturette, or minilecture, provide students with a visual by filling in a semantic map or creating an appropriate graphic organizer emphasizing the lecturette's main ideas and key points. Place the map or organizer on the board. Lecturettes typically last less than seven minutes. (See Strategy 5, Graphic Organizers, Semantic Maps, and Word Webs, for specific examples.)

WHO: Elementary/Middle/High
WHEN: During the lesson
CONTENT AREA(S):   All

• Find and show students a visual or a real artifact to clarify a concept being taught. For example, bring in a live gloxinia as you teach the vocabulary word for this flowering plant, show a picture of the Great Wall of China as you teach about its history, or bring in a pizza to teach the concept of fractional pieces.

WHO: Elementary/Middle/High
WHEN: During the lesson
CONTENT AREA(S):   Mathematics

• Have students come to the chalkboard, dry erase board, overhead, or SMART board and work math problems that can serve as visuals for the remainder of the class. Have them explain the steps in solving the problem so that students have an auditory link to the visual problem.

WHO: Elementary/Middle/High
WHEN: Before the lesson
CONTENT AREA(S):   All

• Place visuals on the classroom bulletin boards and walls that introduce or reinforce concepts being taught. For example, display a visual of the *periodic table* on the wall in a science class or the eight parts of speech in a language arts class.

WHO:	Elementary/Middle/High
WHEN:	After the lesson
CONTENT AREA(S):	All

- Create a *word wall* by categorizing basic sight words and/or content-area vocabulary words and placing them on the wall under the appropriate alphabet letter or by the parts of speech they represent as they are taught.

WHO:	Elementary/Middle/High
WHEN:	During the lesson
CONTENT AREA(S):	History

- During the course of the school year, add specific historical events to a timeline placed around the wall so that students can visually see the relationships between sequential events in history.

WHO:	Elementary/Middle/High
WHEN:	Before the lesson
CONTENT AREA(S):	All

- Prior to reading content-area texts, have students survey the chapter or unit of study and peruse any visuals such as maps, charts, graphs, pictures, chapter titles and subtitles, or bold headings. Have them make predictions as to what the chapter or unit will include. This survey technique, called *SQ3R* (Survey, Question, Read, Recite, Review) should facilitate comprehension.

WHO:	Elementary/Middle/High
WHEN:	During the lesson
CONTENT AREA(S):	All

- Have visuals that do not compete with your lesson. For example, if you show a PowerPoint visual, have a miniature copy of it because students will want to take notes from it rather than listening to you. Be sure your visuals and your voice go together.

WHO:	Elementary/Middle/High
WHEN:	During the lesson
CONTENT AREA(S):	All

- Gain and keep students' visual attention by changing your location in the room. Begin your lesson in the front of the class and then shift to other areas. This tactic will not only keep students interested but also put you in close proximity to all students and communicate to them that you care about their well-being and are interested in what they are doing. *Remember to teach on your feet, not in your seat!*

REFLECTION AND APPLICATION

How will I incorporate *visuals* into instruction to engage students' brains?

Standard/Objective: _____

_____.

Activity: _____

_____.

Standard/Objective: _____

_____.

Activity: _____

_____.

Standard/Objective: _____

_____.

Activity: _____

_____.

Standard/Objective: _____

_____.

Activity: _____

_____.

Standard/Objective: _____

_____.

Activity: _____

_____.

Standard/Objective: _____

_____.

Activity: _____

_____.

Strategy 19

Work Study and Apprenticeships

WHAT: DEFINING THE STRATEGY

Think back to when you finished high school. No doubt you can recall the names of many students in your senior class who did not have the grades or the SAT scores to place in the top 25th or even the 50th percentile of graduating seniors. However, fast-forward to your 10-year class reunion. How many of these so-called nonachievers became extremely successful in the actual world of work? Could it be that much of the knowledge and skill one acquires in school may have little relationship to the actual knowledge and skill required for success in real life? Could it be that for some occupations, on-the-job training may be infinitely more valuable than memorization and regurgitation of isolated facts, which seem to earn the A's in school?

Allow me to relate this story that a high school teacher in one of my classes told me. One of her students whom she taught math barely passed her class. She related that he was fortunate to earn a grade of *D*. Years later, she was having major renovations done on her home and had asked around to find the best construction crew in the city for the job. She was referred to one specific company. Guess who was the head of this company? You guessed it! Her *failing* student. As they talked, he related that measurements and angles in the textbook meant nothing to him until he began to use these concepts in his real-life profession of construction.

Work study, apprenticeships, practicums, and internships may be instructional strategies that afford students the best of both worlds: exposure in school to a wide variety of experiences that help students' determine possible career choices and actual on-the-job work experiences that prepare students for success in the real world.

WHY: THEORETICAL FRAMEWORK

When students are taught to connect new learning to things within their real world, the new learning becomes relevant. (Allen, 2008)

Students should learn that mathematics is an ever-changing subject and that what we learn in school is related to the discoveries of real mathematicians and to everyday life. (Rothstein, Rothstein, & Lauber, 2006)

One of the problems with high schools is their propensity to cover a great deal of content without providing students the opportunity to use that content in the context of authentic situations. (Wiggins & McTighe, 2008)

Students are motivated when teachers show them the connections between mastery in mathematics and their success in other subjects, as well as math's relevance in their daily lives. (Posamentier & Jaye, 2006)

The schoolwork of adolescents must take them into the "dynamic life of their environments." (Brooks, 2002, p. 72)

Educated adults often have difficulty finding a job or meeting job expectations because large gaps can exist between the performance needed to be successful in a business setting and those required for school success. (Sternberg & Grigorenko, 2000)

The strongest neural networks are created when students are actually engaged in real-life experiences and not from tasks that are not authentic. (Westwater & Wolfe, 2000)

Mathematics isn't a scary and abstract mystery when everyday life applications are used to teach it. (Posamentier & Jaye, 2006)

When students learn under the supervision of an expert in the field, they are given full participation in the process of learning and working. (Wonacott, 1993)

Learning should be organized around cognitive-apprenticeship principles that stress subject-specific content and the skills required to function within the content. (Berryman & Bailey, 1992)

When students observe and confer with an expert, they build technical skills and share tasks that relate those technical skills to their knowledge and interpretation. (Wonacott, 1993)

HOW: INSTRUCTIONAL ACTIVITIES

WHO: Middle/High
WHEN: After the lesson
CONTENT AREA(S): All

- There are a number of different instruments that can assess a student's interest in and aptitude for a variety of professions. If the school does not already administer one to students, find one and allow students to take it so that they can begin to think about which professions they may like to pursue.

WHO: Elementary/Middle/High
WHEN: After the lesson
CONTENT AREA(S): All

- As students complete various curricular objectives, invite professionals who use the given skills or knowledge in their daily jobs to speak to the class. For example, as math students complete a chapter on types of angles, have architects demonstrate to the class ways in which angles play a part in building bridges or houses. After these presentations, students are less likely to ask the question, "Why do we have to learn this?"

WHO: Elementary/Middle/High
WHEN: After the lesson
CONTENT AREA(S): All

- Have students research professions of interest and create reports or projects to share what they have learned with the class. In this way, students get to glean information regarding a variety of occupations for future study.

WHO: Middle/High
WHEN: After the lesson
CONTENT AREA(S): All

- Partner with local businesses who can make it possible for students to engage in internships, apprenticeships, and/or work-study projects either during the school year or during the summer months so that they can experience firsthand the knowledge and skills essential for the workplace. Allow them to spend time with professionals who use course content or skills in their daily occupations.

WHO: Elementary/Middle/High
WHEN: During the lesson
CONTENT AREA(S): All

- Engage students in a service-learning project where they are providing a service for their school or community while mastering curriculum. For example, have them beautify the school grounds by planning and implementing a butterfly garden. Have them research the necessary components for the garden, perform the essential measurements of the grounds, and calculate what should be planted where while journaling the entire experience. Service learning is one of the best vehicles for combining interdisciplinary instruction with real-world skills and strategies as well as character.

WHO: Elementary/Middle/High
WHEN: Before, during, or after the lesson
CONTENT AREA(S):   Mathematics

• Have students take turns working as apprentices in the school store to develop the knowledge and skills necessary for successful entrepreneurship.

WHO: Elementary/Middle/High
WHEN: During the lesson
CONTENT AREA(S):   Mathematics

• PBS publishes *The Eddie Files* that documents a student as he learns how professionals use mathematics in the workplace. This resource should be helpful in showing students how productive people use mathematics in their workplace.

WHO: High
WHEN: During the lesson
CONTENT AREA(S):   All

• Introduce students to *schools to work programs*. Consult the Internet for specific details.

WHO: Elementary/Middle/High
WHEN: Before, during, or after the lesson
CONTENT AREA(S):   Mathematics

• Under the direction of a teacher, have students plan and operate a school bank in which fellow students can deposit money. Use this real-life experience to enable students to master math concepts such as bank deposits and withdrawals, interest rates, percentages, and so forth. Have students take turns serving as apprentices in the banking business.

REFLECTION AND APPLICATION

How will I incorporate *work study and apprenticeships* into instruction to engage students' brains?

Standard/Objective: _____

_____

Activity: _____

_____

Standard/Objective: _____

_____

Activity: _____

_____

Standard/Objective: _____

_____

Activity: _____

_____

Standard/Objective: _____

_____

Activity: _____

_____

Standard/Objective: _____

_____

Activity: _____

_____

Standard/Objective: _____

_____

Activity: _____

_____

Writing and Journals

WHAT: DEFINING THE STRATEGY

A teacher related this story to me. She provides a daily opportunity for her students to write in a personal journal. The writing is never graded and students are given the option to have their writing read or not. If students want her to read what they have written, they leave their page in the journal unfolded. If folded, the pages are never read. One day, a sixth grader wrote out her very explicit plans for committing suicide. She did not bother to fold the page, which indicated that she wanted her teacher to read about her plans. As soon as they were read, the teacher immediately obtained help for the obviously troubled student.

Writing not only helps students express their emotions in a constructive way but also assists students in retaining content. Have you ever written a list of groceries that you wanted to purchase at the store and then forgotten to take the list with you? Isn't it ironic that you can recall the majority of items on the list?

Writing is cross-curricular and should be encouraged in every content area. However, when the word *writing* is mentioned, teachers often think only of the full completion of the writing process: prewriting, writing, proofreading, revising, and rewriting. However, *quick writes* enable students to use this crucial skill in a multitude of cross-curricular ways for short periods.

WHY: THEORETICAL FRAMEWORK

Journals enable teachers to focus students' attention toward the content, monitor students' understanding of the content, and allow them to freely express their ideas without embarrassment. (Algozzine, Campbell, & Wang, 2009b)

Journal writing assists the brain in making meaning out of the new information it acquires. (Jensen, 2007)

Rubrics created and scored by students enable them to focus their writing and think more critically about it. (Algozzine et al., 2009b)

The best way to recall an experience in detail is to write down an account of it right after it happens. (Markowitz & Jensen, 2007)

The following framework should be adhered to when teaching students with learning disabilities to write: (1) providing students with a planning think sheet, (2) helping them create a first draft, and (3) incorporating a peer-coaching approach for revising and editing. (Sousa, 2007)

Writing enables the brain to reverse the reading process. Rather than responding initially to external visual stimuli, during the writing process, the brain starts with internal thoughts, chooses appropriate vocabulary to express those thoughts, and then produces the symbols for the words in writing. (Wolfe & Nevills, 2004)

Having students write notes or copy them from the board while the teacher continues talking can be a distraction. (Jensen & Nickelsen, 2008)

When the kinesthetic activity of writing is used to communicate math concepts, more neurons are engaged and students are made to organize their thoughts. (Sousa, 2007)

When students were given written model solutions (examples that had been worked out) to refer to when solving practice problems, they made fewer errors than a comparable group who solved a greater number of practice problems without the written model solutions. (Posamentier & Jaye, 2006)

Journal writing can be done at every grade level and content area and increases retention and positive transfer of information. (Sousa, 2006)

Prekindergarten through second-grade students should be encouraged to use paper and pencil to record what they are thinking when solving computational problems. (National Council of Teachers of Mathematics, 2000)

When students are taught to form images in their minds while reading, their writing can be positively affected. (Miller, 2002)

Having students write down what is observed, presented, or thought about helps the brain organize and make sense of extremely complicated and multifaceted bits of information. (Jensen, 2000)

Students should be encouraged to talk and write about their ideas, to comprehend the basic concepts being taught, and to put those concepts into their own words. (Kohn, 1999)

HOW: INSTRUCTIONAL ACTIVITIES

WHO:	Elementary/Middle/High
WHEN:	During the lesson
CONTENT AREA(S):	All

• When expecting students to take notes or write down meaningful parts of your lecture, provide time for them to do so. Either have them write first and then continue talking or talk first and then give them time to write. Otherwise, many students miss key points.

WHO:	Elementary/Middle/High
WHEN:	During the lesson
CONTENT AREA(S):	All

• Give students many opportunities to write for a variety of real-world, cross-curricular purposes. Reasons for writing should include the following: to inform, to persuade, to express, and to entertain. For example, have students write an essay about one event that changed the course of their lives. Watch the emotional reaction that this activity can engender!

WHO:	Elementary/Middle/High
WHEN:	During the lesson
CONTENT AREA(S):	Mathematics

• Give students a variety of medium that provide them with opportunities to express their ideas in writing. These could include, but are not limited to, posters, brochures, scripts for plays, book jackets, commercials, and graphic organizers. Consult Chapter 5: Graphic Organizers, Semantic Maps, and Word Webs for examples of various mind maps.

WHO:	Elementary/Middle/High
WHEN:	During the lesson
CONTENT AREA(S):	Language arts

• Expand students' reading and writing vocabularies by identifying *tired words* that are over used in students' writing, such as *said, like, good,* and *pretty.* Have students brainstorm a list of synonyms that give them alternative vocabulary words to make their writing more interesting and appealing. For example, for the word *said,* the brainstormed list could include *replied, exclaimed, declared,* and *stated.* Compile a class list of alternative words and post it on the wall in class for students to use during future writing assignments. Forbid students to use the tired words and have them incorporate the new words appropriately into their writing.

WHO:	Elementary/Middle/High
WHEN:	During the lesson
CONTENT AREA(S):	All

- Have students use the concept of *SUPED-UP learning* during the writing process. *SUPED* is an acronym for the following:

S   After providing a model on how to write a **summary** paragraph, have students write a five- to eight-sentence summary paragraph.

U   Have them **underline** important ideas from the summary while writing questions to be answered in the margins,

P   Have students' **peers** edit what they have written.

E   Have students **edit** their original summary and revise it based on the oral or written feedback from peers.

D   Place students in groups of four to six and hold a **discussion** with a leader and a list of questions (Jensen, 2009b).

WHO:	Elementary/Middle/High
WHEN:	During the lesson
CONTENT AREA(S):	Mathematics

- Have students write the steps when solving computational or word problems. Not only will the written steps assist the student in remembering the sequence of the solution but will also provide insight into the thinking of the student during problem solving.

WHO:	Elementary/Middle/High
WHEN:	During the lesson
CONTENT AREA(S):	All

- As you present a lecturette (a minilecture of five to seven minutes), have students write key concepts and phrases that will help them remember your content. Be sure to give them time to write so that their brains will not have to engage in two behaviors simultaneously—listening to your continued talk and trying to remember what to write.

WHO:	Elementary/Middle/High
WHEN:	During the lesson
CONTENT AREA(S):	All

- Incorporate *Quick Writes* throughout a lesson. Stop periodically during the lesson and have students write a concept just taught. Writing, even for a minute will help to reinforce the content. For example, stop your lesson and tell students the following: "Write the steps in the scientific process? Write the three causes of the Civil War?"

WHO:	Elementary/Middle/High
WHEN:	During the lesson
CONTENT AREA(S):	All

- Have students carry a piece of writing through the following five stages of the writing process for publication in a class book.

- o **Prewriting**—Have students brainstorm a jot list of ideas regarding an original composition or related to an assigned topic.
- o **Writing**—Have students write a rough draft of the composition according to teacher guidelines.
- o **Editing**—Have student assess one another's writing according to a rubric developed by the class.
- o **Revising**—Have students revise their composition in light of peer feedback from the rubric.
- o **Final Draft**—Have student produce a written or typed final draft that is ready for publication in the class book.

WHO:	Elementary/Middle/High
WHEN:	During the lesson
CONTENT AREA(S):	All

- In an effort to improve the students' quality of journal writing, have them brainstorm an *alphabet book* that would include vocabulary chunked according to the letters of the alphabet, yet pertinent to a unit of study. For example, during a unit of geometry, a *geometry alphabet book* could look like the following: *acute, base, circumference, diameter, equilateral, figure*, and so forth. Post these words as a visual or have students include them in their notebooks for ready reference.

WHO:	Elementary/Middle/High
WHEN:	After the lesson
CONTENT AREA(S):	All

- Following a unit of study in any content area, have students record their thoughts regarding the unit in their personal journals. The following open-ended question starters may serve to spark the thinking of students:

  - o State at least three major concepts you learned in this unit.
  - o What was your favorite activity in which the class participated?
  - o What was your least favorite activity in which the class participated?
  - o How can you apply what you have learned to your personal life or to a future career choice?
  - o If this unit were taught again, what things would you change?

WHO:	Elementary/Middle/High
WHEN:	During or after the lesson
CONTENT AREA(S):	All

- Provide time daily for students to write in a personal journal regarding topics of choice including descriptions of incidents that have happened at home, personal reflections on class assignments, or feeling or emotions expressed. Journals are not graded and students can indicate whether they want their entries read by the teacher by leaving the page unfolded if it is to be read or folding the page lengthwise if it is not to be read.

REFLECTION AND APPLICATION

How will I incorporate *writing and journals* into instruction to engage students' brains?

Standard/Objective: _____

_____

Activity: _____

_____

Standard/Objective: _____

_____

Activity: _____

_____

Standard/Objective: _____

_____

Activity: _____

_____

Standard/Objective: _____

_____

Activity: _____

_____

Standard/Objective: _____

_____

Activity: _____

_____

Standard/Objective: _____

_____

Activity: _____

_____

Resource

Brain-Compatible Lesson Design

In the first edition of this book, I had not yet conceived the idea of a brain-compatible lesson plan, which would integrate the 20 strategies directly into instruction. Now I have! An adaptation of this plan is currently being used nationwide as school systems revise curriculum and ensure that teachers are planning lessons that not only maximize student achievement and help students meet content standards. They also go a long way toward enabling students to retain the content long after the examinations are over. The plan answers the following question: *How can I incorporate the 20 brain-compatible strategies into my daily lesson plans?* A sample lesson plan is displayed on page 148.

It does not matter to me whether you use the lesson plan form as you put your lessons together. What does matter is whether you can honestly ask and answer the five questions on the plan that are delineated in the paragraphs that follow.

SECTION 1: LESSON OBJECTIVE: WHAT WILL YOU BE TEACHING? ■

Obviously, when teachers are planning lessons, the first question they should ask themselves should be, *What will I be teaching?* This question is answered by examining content curriculum, which addresses local, state, and national standards. As I travel the country, teachers express their frustration at being asked to teach more and more content every year with nothing being deleted. They tell me that they would like to incorporate the strategies during instruction, but they simply do not have the time. And yet when I travel to other countries, many of which outscore us on achievement tests, *less appears to be more*. Their textbooks are about one-third the size of ours, and content is chunked together into relevant concepts to be taught. Why can't we in the United States look at our content that way?

I pray that the days are gone when teachers have students open the textbook to page one at the beginning of the school year and conclude instruction with the last page of the book prior to summer vacation. The days should be over when teaching social studies consist solely of round-robin oral reading the chapter as the class follows along in their textbook and then having the class answer the questions at the end of the chapter. Content may be covered but retention is limited!

A better way of teaching calls for a paradigm shift on the part of many professionals who look at their subject matter as content to be covered or isolated skills to be mastered. Madeline Hunter, a noted educator, said it best, "If all you are doing is covering content, then get a shovel and cover it with dirt because it is dead to the memory of your students." So as you answer the question, *What will I be teaching?* examine your curriculum for concepts that can be chunked or connected together and realize that the textbook is only one of many tools for teaching those concepts. When I am asked to deliver a model lesson in a classroom, more times than not, I do not use the textbook. There are so many other options for engaging my students. After all, you don't have to read the entire chapter on the Civil War to know the causes of it!

Let's look again at Scenario II in the Introduction of this text. If you remember, students in Mr. Stewart's class are expected to know the branches of the federal government, the function of each branch, and what positions are included in each branch. That is his lesson objective and answers the question, *What will he be teaching?* Why don't we use this lesson and carry it through the brain-compatible lesson plan questions that follow?

◾ SECTION 2: ASSESSMENT: HOW WILL YOU KNOW STUDENTS HAVE LEARNED THE CONTENT?

When planning a lesson, if you wait until the completion of the plan to decide how you will assess your students, you have actually waited too long. I can still visualize myself as a student in school. I remember being stressed on test days because assessment sometimes meant trying to guess what my teachers were going to put on their tests. If I guessed correctly, I would manage to make an *A*. However, if I guessed incorrectly, even if I studied feverishly, my grade was not so good. The current research tells us to *begin with the end in mind*. Tell students what you expect. Your expectations should not be kept a secret. What should students know and be able to do at the culmination of a lesson or unit of study? In this way, your assessment may be a challenge to the brains of students, but not a high stressor. Consider this analogy. How can a pilot file his or her flight plan without knowing the destination? Tell students their destination, and they will stand a better chance of getting there.

In our example, students in Mr. Stewart's class were told that by the culmination of the lesson, they should be able to name the three branches of the federal government, tell what each branch does, and determine what positions are included in each branch.

SECTION 3: WAYS TO GAIN/MAINTAIN ATTENTION: HOW WILL YOU GAIN AND MAINTAIN STUDENTS' ATTENTION?

(Consider need, novelty, meaning, and emotion)

There is so much stimuli in the world that brains are very particular regarding what they choose to pay attention to. When you are teaching, you are vying for a spot in the brains of your students. But your lesson may be competing with the conversation of a peer, a noise in the hall, a colorful leaf on a tree outside the window, or reflections of an argument that the student had with his parent before he came to school. Students can even be staring you in the face and not paying a bit of attention to what you are teaching.

There are four major ways to gain your students' attention. Mr. Stewart has the benefit of using all four ways. Do you have to grab students' attention using all four ways in every lesson? Absolutely not! Do you have to grab students' attention using at least one way? Absolutely so! The ways are *need, novelty, meaning,* and *emotion.*

Need

The first way to grab the attention of your students is through need. When students do not see the need of learning what you are teaching, they just may not pay attention. If students see the purpose in what you are teaching, they will see the need to learn it. For example, my son struggled in high school because he has characteristics of attention deficit disorder and many of his teachers at the middle and high school levels did not engage his brain during instruction. After he graduated, he did not see the *need* to go to college, so he began working a job. After several years of not making the salary he thought he deserved and not having his talents utilized, he came to us and told us he now saw the need to go to college. Since he enrolled, he has done very well. Why? Need is a big motivator for the brain.

When students see the purpose for your lesson, they will see the need to learn the content. Simply telling them that they will need the information for a subsequent test may not be enough motivation for many students. In our sample lesson, Mr. Stewart gave students a purpose. They would need to know how the government functions so that when they are old enough to cast their ballot for local, state, and national leaders, they can cast an informed ballot.

Novelty

Sometimes need is simply not sufficient for engaging students in the lesson. You may know that your students need the information but your students don't share your sense of urgency. The good news is that you have three more ways to gain their attention. A second way is by teaching your content in a *novel* and interesting way. The brain tends to pay attention to things in the environment that are new or different. For example, at one time we lived in a subdivision near a railroad track. Before we purchased our home, I asked potential neighbors if they heard the train as it passed. They told me no and assured me that the noise from the train would not be a problem should we decide to live in the neighborhood. Well, I'm sure you can guess what happened! We subsequently bought the house and during the first two to three weeks, I heard the trains each and every time they passed the subdivision. I was actually agitated that the neighbors had lied to me. Well, that lasted for less than a month. Soon, the noise from the train was not novel anymore, and I paid little or no attention to it.

While you certainly want consistency in your class rituals and procedures, you will want to vary your lesson delivery. When you change your location in the room, your voice inflection, or the strategies you use to deliver your lesson, you are being novel, and you stand a better chance of gaining and maintaining your students' attention.

The 20 strategies provide you with many ways to be novel. Think of all the novel stories you and your students can tell, the variety of songs you can play, the projects in which you can engage your students, all the different movements you can use to put information into procedural memory. The options are endless!

In our sample lesson, Mr. Stewart uses the activities of having students draw a graphic organizer delineating the branches of the government and having them role-play as if they belonged to that branch as novel ways to introduce students to the concept. The lesson is truly different and much more engaging than round-robin oral reading of the chapter and answering questions at the end of it!

Meaning

Because the brain's purpose is survival in the real world, when you are connecting your content to real life, you are making it meaningful. When you are not, students will raise their hands and ask this question: Why do we have to learn this? As I teach, I take every opportunity to use real-life examples to illustrate my points. When I tell students the true story about the fact that my father had the trait for sickle-cell anemia and how that trait has been passed on to my sister and her daughter, that story goes a long way toward giving my science lesson on dominant and recessive genes more meaning. When teachers have students write about one decision that they made that changed the course of their lives, the writing lesson becomes unforgettable!

It is very meaningful when Mr. Stewart structures his lesson so that students are assuming roles that they may one day actually assume as a part of the federal government. What stronger connection to real life can there be?

Emotion

Of all the ways to gain and maintain students' attention, emotion may be the most powerful! Emotion places experiences in reflexive memory, one of the strongest memory systems in the brain and helps to ensure retention. In fact, you will not soon forget anything that happened to you in your personal life or in the world at large that was emotional. I bet you can even remember where you were when it happened. For example, where were you on January 28, 1986, when you were informed that the *Challenger* had exploded? I used to use the example of the assassination of President John F. Kennedy but teachers are so young now that few were even born when that fateful day occurred.

Teachers who are emotional about their content are passionate and enthusiastic! My daughter Jessica had an English teacher who was passionate about Edgar Allan Poe. She so intrigued my daughter that soon Jessica was reading everything that Poe wrote. No doubt, you remember a math teacher who made you love math or a science teacher whose hands-on lessons were unforgettable!

In our example, Mr. Stewart's lesson was fun and motivating. As he went around the room *anointing people with power* with his magic wand, students laughed and quickly went to the corner that was representative of the branch in which they belonged. The lesson was highly engaging and the positive emotion was obvious.

Need, novelty, meaning, and emotion are four ways to gain the brain's attention. You do not need to have all four working for you in one lesson. Even one, used appropriately, will work as you compete with the multitude of stimuli surrounding your students during your lesson presentation.

SECTION 4: CONTENT CHUNKS: HOW WILL YOU DIVIDE AND TEACH THE CONTENT TO ENGAGE STUDENTS' BRAINS?

Many years ago, a guru in the field of education by the name of Madeline Hunter asked another question, *How do you eat an elephant?* The answer of course was *one bite at a time.* The adult brain can only hold approximately seven bits of information (plus or minus two) simultaneously, which is why there are seven days in a week, numbers in a phone number, colors in the rainbow, notes on the scale, wonders of the ancient world, continents, dwarfs, and so forth. The way to get the brain to remember more content would be to connect or chunk it together. This is why the social security number, which is more than seven digits, is in chunks. It is nine digits and, therefore, needs to be connected together into three chunks. A telephone number with an area code is 10 digits. However, it is also divided into three chunks to make it easier for you to remember. You see, the brain remembers a chunk as if it were one piece of information, rather than separate numbers.

In our sample lesson, the objective was first divided into the following three smaller chunks: (1) judicial branch, (2) executive branch, and (3) legislative branch.

I have added another question to Madeline Hunter's question, *How do you digest an elephant?* The answer of course is that you have to *chew it up*. Activity enables the brain to *chew up* information. Chew is a metaphor for the fact that the activity enables the brain to process or *digest* what it is learning. A classroom where there is little opportunity for students to process what they are learning is a classroom where students are not performing at optimal levels and may not be comprehending or retaining as much as you would like.

Mr. Stewart used several different activities as he taught each of the three branches. As he taught the judicial branch, he connected the *J* in *judicial* to the fact that this branch *judges* the laws, and he drew a mind map on the board as he told who was in this branch. He asked the students to draw the mind map on their paper for later reference. When he had finished with this first chunk, Mr. Stewart asked students to reteach their partners what he had just taught about the first branch. After all, we learn 90% of what we teach to others.

Chunk 2 consisted of teaching about the *executive* branch who *executes* the laws. I hope you see the relationship in the letter *E*. The graphic organizer was expanded to include this branch, and students answered questions orally as they were asked by Mr. Stewart.

Chunk 3 dealt with the *legislative* branch, which makes the *laws*. This branch was included in the mind map with the accompanying positions.

The role play that followed enabled students to connect all three branches as students were assigned roles and asked to report to the branch in which they belonged. A discussion ensued.

The lesson was closed with a review of the major concepts gleaned from the lesson. This review was *clothed* in a ball game where students were giving answers after catching a ball.

■ SECTION 5: BRAIN-COMPATIBLE STRATEGIES: WHICH WILL YOU USE TO DELIVER CONTENT?

By the time a teacher completes a lesson plan, the activities included in the lesson should reflect the 20 brain-compatible strategies outlined in this book. In fact, on the bottom of the sample lesson-plan form, all 20 strategies are listed so that teachers have a ready reference for their use.

In every lesson I teach, regardless of which grade level or content area, I attempt to incorporate at least four of the strategies, one from each of the four modalities: visual, auditory, kinesthetic, and tactile. (Refer to Figure 0.1 in the Introduction for a correlation of the strategies to the learning modalities.) In this way, regardless of student preferences, there is an activity in the lesson for every student and instruction can be differentiated based on students' learning needs.

In our sample lesson, the strategies used to teach the objective included the following: *graphic organizers* (he drew a mind map on the board of the branches of the government); *visuals* (the mind map served as a visual for the class); *mnemonic devices* (connections were made between the letters in the function and the name of the branch); *reciprocal teaching* (students retaught what they had learned about the government to their close partner); *role play* (students assumed roles in the federal government); *movement* (students got up and went to the branch of government in which they belonged); *discussion* (the class discussed whether students had reported to the correct branch); and *games* (students caught the ball and provided answers during an ending review). By the time this lesson ended, every student knew the branches of the government and who was in what branch, and at least 8 of the 20 brain-compatible strategies had been incorporated.

If you come to the end of a lesson plan and have not utilized any of the brain-compatible strategies, go back and plan it again. It is not brain-compatible! We must begin to teach smarter, and not harder. Teaching smarter means the following:

1. Teaching the major content chunks that students need to know

2. Letting students know what is expected of them at the beginning of the lesson

3. Utilizing ways to gain and maintain the attention of students at the beginning of the lesson (because students tend to remember what happens first in your lesson) as well as throughout the lesson

4. Deciding how many different chunks are needed to get students through the content

5. Incorporating brain-compatible strategies into the activities designed to teach each chunk of information

BRAIN-COMPATIBLE LESSON PLAN

Lesson Objective(s): *What will you be teaching?*

Assessment (Traditional/Authentic): *How will you know students have learned the content?*

Ways to Gain/Maintain Attention (Primacy): *How will you gain and maintain students' attention? Consider need, novelty, meaning, or emotion.*

Content Chunks: *How will you divide and teach the content to engage students' brains?*

Lesson Segment 1:

Activities:

Lesson Segment 2:

Activities:

Lesson Segment 3:

Activities:

Brain-Compatible Strategies: *Which will you use to deliver content?*

- ☐ Brainstorming/Discussion
- ☐ Drawing/Artwork
- ☐ Field Trips
- ☐ Games
- ☐ Graphic Organizers/Semantic Maps/Word Webs
- ☐ Humor
- ☐ Manipulatives/Experiments/Labs/ Models
- ☐ Metaphor/Analogy/Simile
- ☐ Mnemonic Devices
- ☐ Movement
- ☐ Music/Rhythm/Rhyme/Rap
- ☐ Project/Problem-Based Instruction
- ☐ Reciprocal Teaching/Cooperative Learning
- ☐ Roleplay/Drama/Pantomime/Charades
- ☐ Storytelling
- ☐ Technology
- ☐ Visualization/Guided Imagery
- ☐ Visuals
- ☐ Work Study/Apprenticeships
- ☐ Writing/Journals

Bibliography

Access Center. (2004, October 1). Retrieved August 31, 2009 from http://coe .jme.edu/mathvidsr/disabilities.htm.

Allen, R. H. (2002). *Impact teaching: Ideas and strategies for teachers to maximize student learning*. Boston: Allyn & Bacon.

Allen, R. (2008). *Green light classrooms: Teaching techniques that accelerate learning*. Victoria, Australia: Hawker Brownlow.

Algozzine, B., Campbell, P., & Wang, A. (2009a). *63 tactics for teaching diverse learners: Grades K–6*. Thousand Oaks: CA: Corwin.

Algozzine, B., Campbell, P., & Wang, A. (2009b). *63 tactics for teaching diverse learners: Grades 6–12*. Thousand Oaks: CA: Corwin.

Anderson, L. W., & Krathwohl, D. R. (2001). *A taxonomy for learning, teaching, and assessing*. New York: Addison Wesley Longman.

Art Junction. (n.d.). *Drawing encounters*. Retrieved August 20, 2009, from http://artjunction.org/encounters_drawing.php.

Barr, R. D., & Parrett, W. (2007). *Saving our students, saving our schools: 50 proven strategies for helping*. Thousand Oaks: CA: Corwin.

Bayer, J. (1984). *A, my name is Alice*. New York: Dial Books for Young Readers.

Bender, W. (2005). *Differentiating math instruction: Strategies that work for K–8 classrooms!* Thousand Oaks, CA: Corwin.

Berryman, S. E., & Bailey, T. R. (1992). *The double helix of education and the economy*. New York: Institute on Education and the Economy, Columbia University Teachers College.

Bloom, B. S. (Ed.). (1956). *Taxonomy of educational objectives. The classification of educational goals, by a committee of college and university examiners*. New York: Longmans.

Brooks, J. (2002). *Schooling for life*. Alexandria, VA: Association for Supervision and Curriculum Development.

Brooks, J., & Brooks, M. (1993). *In search of understanding: The case for constructivist classrooms*. Alexandria, VA: Association for Supervision and Curriculum Development.

Budd, J. W. (2004). Mind maps as classroom exercises. *Journal of Economic Education, 35*(1), 35–46.

Bulla, D. (1996). *Think math! Interactive loops for groups*. Chicago: Zephyr Press.

Burgess, R. (2000). *Laughing lessons: 1492/3 ways to make teaching and learning fun*. Minneapolis, MN: Free Spirit.

Caine, R. N., Caine, G., McClintic, C., & Klimek, K. (2005). *12 brain/mind learning principles in action: The fieldbook for making connections, teaching, and the human brain*. Victoria, Australia: Hawker Brownlow.

Catterall, J., Chapleau, R., & Iwanga, J. (1999, Fall). *Involvement in the arts and human development: Extending an analysis of general associations and introducing the special cases of intense involvement in music and in theater arts* (Monograph Series No. 11). Washington, DC: Americas for the Arts.

Checkley, K. (1999). *Math in the early grades: Laying a foundation for later learning*. Alexandria, VA: Association for Supervision and Curriculum Development.

Children's Health Education Center. (n.d.). *Educational benefits of field trips.* [Electronic version]. Retrieved August 21, 2009, from http://www.bluekids.org/health_education/benefit-of-field-trip.asp.

Coggins, D., Kravin, D., Coates, G. D., & Carrol, M. D. (2007). *English language learners in the mathematics classroom.* Thousand Oaks, CA: Corwin.

Coleman, E., Rivkin, I., & Brown, A. (1997). The effect of instructional explanations on learning from scientific texts. *Journal of the Learning Sciences, 6,* 347–365.

Costa, A. L. (1991). *Teaching for intelligent behavior: Outstanding strategies for strengthening your students' thinking skills.* Bellevue, WA: Bureau of Education and Research.

Costa, A. L. (2008). *The school as a home for the mind: Creating mindful curriculum, instruction, and dialogue* (2nd ed.). Victoria, Australia: Hawker Brownlow Education.

Covey, S. (1996). *The seven habits of highly effective people.* Salt Lake City, UT: Covey Leadership Center.

Curtain-Phillips, M. (2008). *How to make the most of math manipulatives—A fresh look at getting students' heads and hands around math concepts.* Retrieved August 31, 2009, from http://www.mathgoodies.com/articles/ manipulatives.html.

Davis, L. (2002). *The importance of field trips.* Retrieved August 21, 2009, http://gsa.confex.com.gsa/2002RM/finalprogram/abstract_33868.htr.

Defina, P. (2003). *The neurobiology of memory: Understand, apply, and assess student memory.* Paper presented at the Learning and the Brain Conference, Cambridge, MA.

Deshler, D., & Schmaker, J. (2006). *Teaching adolescents with disabilities: Accessing the general education curriculum.* Thousand Oaks, CA: Corwin.

Dewey, J. (1934). *Art as experience.* New York: Minion Ballet.

Dewey, J. (1938). *Experience and education.* New York: Macmillan.

Drake, S. (1996). Guided imagery and education. Theory, practice, and experience. *Journal of Mental Imagery, 20,* 1–58.

Ekwall, E. E., & Shanker, J. L. (1988). *Diagnosis and remediation of the disabled reader* (3rd ed.). Boston: Allyn and Bacon.

Feinstein, S. (2004). *Secrets of the teenage brain: Research-based strategies for reaching and teaching today's adolescents.* Thousand Oaks, CA: Corwin.

Fogarty, R. (2001). *Making sense of the research on the brain and learning.* Victoria, Australia: Hawker Brownlow Education.

Gardner, H. (1983). *Frames of mind: The theory of multiple intelligences.* New York: Basic Books.

Gettinger, M., & Kohler, K. M. (2006). Process-outcome approaches to classroom management and effective teaching. In C. Evertson, C. M. Weinstein, & C. S. Weinstein (Eds.), *Handbook of classroom management: Research, practice, and contemporary issues* (pp. 73–95). Mahwah, NJ: Erlbaum.

Gijbels, D., Dochy, F., Van den Bossche, P., & Segers, M. (2005). Effects of problem-based learning. A meta-analysis from the angle of assessment. *Review of Educational Research, 75*(1), 27–61.

Glasser, W. (1990). *The quality school: Managing students without coercion.* New York: HarperCollins.

Glasser, W. (1999). *Choice theory: A new psychology of personal freedom.* New York: HarperCollins.

Goldberg, C. (2004). Brain friendly techniques: Mind mapping. *School Library Media Activities Monthly, 21*(3), 22–24.

Gregory, G., & Chapman, C. (2002). *Differentiated instruction: One size doesn't fit all.* Thousand Oaks, CA: Corwin.

Gregory, G. H., & Parry, T. (2006). *Designing brain-compatible learning* (3rd ed.). Thousand Oaks, CA: Corwin.

Guerrero, S., Walker, N., & Dugdale, S. (2004, spring). Technology in support of middle-grade mathematics: What have we learned? *Journal of Computers in Mathematics and Science Teaching, 23,* 5–20.

Hannaford, C. (2005). *Smart moves: Why learning is not all in your head.* Arlington, VA: Great River Books.

Hiraoka, L. (2006, March 13). All this talk about tech. *NEA Today, 24,* 6.

Hunter, R. (2004). *Madeline Hunter's mastery teaching: Increasing instructional effectiveness in elementary and secondary schools.* Thousand Oaks, CA: Corwin.

India Parenting. (2009). *The benefits of art and your child.* Retrieved August 20, 2009, from http://www.indiaparenting.com/develop/data/develop17_17 .shtml.

Jensen, E. (1995). *Brain-based learning & teaching.* Del Mar, CA: The Brain Store.

Jensen, E. (2000). Moving with the brain in mind. *Educational Leadership, 58*(3), 34–37.

Jensen, E. (2001). *Arts with the brain in mind.* Alexandria, VA: Association for Supervision and Curriculum Development.

Jensen, E. (2002). *Learning with the body in mind.* Thousand Oaks, CA: Corwin.

Jensen, E. (2005). *Top tunes for teaching: 977 song titles and practical tools for choosing the right music every time.* Thousand Oaks, CA: Corwin.

Jensen, E. (2007). *Brain-compatible strategies* (2nd ed.). Victoria Australia: Hawker Brownlow Education.

Jensen, E. (2008). *Brain-based learning: The new paradigm of teaching.* Thousand Oaks, CA: Corwin.

Jensen, E. (2009a). *Fierce teaching: Purpose, passion, and what matters most.* Thousand Oaks, CA: Corwin.

Jensen, E. (2009b). *Super teaching* (4th ed.). Thousand Oaks, CA: Corwin.

Jensen, E., & Dabney, M. (2000). *Learning smarter: The new science of teaching.* San Diego, CA: The Brain Store.

Jensen, E., & Nickelson, L. (2008). *Deeper learning: 7 powerful strategies for in-depth and longer-lasting learning.* Victoria, Australia. Hawker Brownlow.

Jones, C. (2008). *The magic of metaphor.* Retrieved August 10, 2009, from http://www.Uxmatters.com/mt/archives/2008/php.

Kagan, S., & Kagan, M. (2007). *Multiple intelligences: The complete MI book.* Victoria, Australia. Hawker Brownlow Education.

Karten, T. J. (2007). *Inclusion strategies that work!* Victoria, Australia: Hawker Brownlow Education.

Karten, T. J. (2008). *More inclusion strategies that work!* Victoria, Australia: Hawker Brownlow Education.

Karten, T. J. (2009). *Inclusion strategies that work for adolescent learners.* Thousand Oaks, CA: Corwin.

Kohn, A. (1999). *The schools our children deserve: Moving beyond traditional classrooms and tougher standards.* Boston: Houghton Mifflin.

Krepel, W. J., & Duvall, C. R. (1981). *Field trips: A guide for planning and conducting educational experiences.* Washington, DC: National Education Association.

Kuhlmann, S., Kirschbaum, C., & Wolf, O. T. (2005, March). Effects of oral cortisol treatment in healthy young women on memory retrieval of negative and neutral words. *Neurobiology of Learning and Memory, 83,* 158–162.

Lakoff, G., & Johnson, M. (1980). *Metaphors we live by.* Chicago: University of Chicago Press.

LeBoutillier, N., & Marks, D. F. (2003, February). Mental imagery and creativity: A meta-analytic review study. *British Journal of Psychology, 94,* 29–44.

Lieberman, A., & Miller, L. (2000). *Teaching and teacher development: A new synthesis for a new century.* In R. S. Brandt (Ed.), *Education in a new era.* Alexandria, VA: Association for Supervision and Curriculum Development.

Mahoney, S. (2005, July/August). How to live longer. *American Association of Retired People, 48*(4B), 64–72.

Markowitz, K., & Jensen, E. (2007). *The great memory book.* Heatherton, Victoria, Australia: Hawker Brownlow Education.

Marzano, R. J. (2003). *What works in schools: Translating research into action* Alexandria, VA: Association for Supervision and Curriculum Development.

Marzano, R. J. (2007). *The art and science of teaching.* Alexandria, VA: Association for Supervision and Curriculum Development.

Marzano, R. J., Pickering, D. J., & Pollack, J. E. (2001). *Classroom instruction that works.* Alexandria, VA: Association for Supervision and Curriculum Development.

Mayer, R. E. (2003). *Learning and instruction.* Upper Saddle River, NJ: Merrill.

McCormick Tribune Foundation. (Producer). (2004). *What every child needs* [DVD]. Chicago: Chicago Production Center.

McCarthy, B. (1990). Using the 4MAT system to bring learning styles to schools. *Educational Leadership, 48*(2), 31–37.

Miller, D. (2002). *Reading with meaning: Teaching comprehension in the primary grades.* Portland, ME: Stenhouse.

Moskowitz, G., & Hayman, J. L. (1976). Success strategies of inner-city teachers: A year-long study. *Journal of Educational Research, 69,* 283–289.

National Council of Teachers of Mathematics. (Eds.). (2000). *Principles and standards for school mathematics.* Reston, VA: Author.

Nuthall, G. (1999). The way students learn: Acquiring knowledge from an integrated science and social studies unit. *The Elementary School Journal, 99*(4), 303–341.

Ogle, D. M. (2000). Make it visual: A picture is worth a thousand words. In M. McLaughlin & M. Vogt (Eds.), *Creativity and innovation in content area teaching.* Norwood, MA: Christopher-Gordon.

Palincsar, A. S., & Brown, A. L. (1984). Reciprocal teaching in comprehension-fostering and comprehension-monitoring activities. *Cognition and Instruction, 1*(2), 117–175.

Paulin, M. G. (2005). Evolutionary origins and principles of distributed neural computation for state estimation and movement control in vertebrates. *Complexity, 10*(3), 56–65.

Posamentier, A. S., & Hauptman, H. A. (2006). *101+ great ideas for introducing key concepts in mathematics: A resource for secondary school teachers* (2nd ed.). Thousand Oaks, CA: Corwin.

Posamentier, A. S., & Jaye, D. (2006). *What successful math teachers do, Grades 6–12: 79 research-based strategies for the standards-based classroom.* Thousand Oaks, CA: Corwin.

Prystay, C. (2004, December 13). As math skills slip, U. S. schools seek answers from Asia. *The Wall Street Journal,* pp. A1–A8.

Ronis, D. L. (2006). *Brain-compatible mathematics* (2nd ed.). Thousand Oaks, CA: Corwin.

Rothstein, A. S., Rothstein, E., & Lauber, G. (2006). *Write for mathematics* (2nd ed.). Thousand Oaks, CA: Corwin.

Sebesta, L. M., & Martin, S. R. M. (2004). *Fractions: Building a foundation with concrete manipulatives.* Illinois Schools Journal, 83(2), 3–23.

Secretary's Commission on Achieving Necessary Skills. (1991). *What work requires of schools: A SCANS report for America 2000.* Washington, DC: US Department of Labor.

Sheffield, C. (2007, summer). Technology and the gifted adolescent: Higher order thinking, 21st century literacy, and the digital native. *Meridan: A Middle School Computer Technologies Journal, 10(2).* [Electronic version] Retrieved August 15, 2008, from http://www.ncsu.edu/meridian/sum2007.

Sousa, D. (2001). *How the brain learns* (2nd ed.). Thousand Oaks, CA: Corwin.

Sousa, D. A. (2006). *How the brain learns* (3rd ed.). Thousand Oaks, CA: Corwin.

Sousa, D. A. (2007). *How the special needs brain learns* (2nd ed.). Thousand Oaks CA: Corwin.

Sprenger, M. (1999). *Learning and memory: The brain in action.* Alexandria, VA: Association for Supervision and Curriculum Development.

Sprenger, M. (2007a). *Becoming a "wiz" at brain-based teaching: How to make every year your best year* (2nd ed.). Thousand Oaks, CA: Corwin.

Sprenger, M. (2007b). *Memory 101 for educators.* Thousand Oaks, CA: Corwin.

Sternberg, R. J., & Grigorenko, E. L. (2000). *Teaching for successful intelligence: To increase student learning and achievement.* Arlington Heights, IL: Skylight.

Storm, B. (1999). The enhanced imagination: Storytelling? Power to entrance listeners. *Storytelling, 2*(2).

Thornburgh, N. (2006). Dropout nation. [Special edition]. *TIME, 167*(16).

Tileston, D. W. (2004). *Training manual for what every teacher should know.* Thousand Oaks, CA: Corwin.

Udvari-Solner, A., & Kluth, P. (2008). *Joyful learning: Active and collaborative learning in inclusive classrooms.* Thousand Oaks, CA: Corwin.

Wall, E. S., & Posamentier, A. S. (2006). *What successful math teachers do, Grades PreK–5: 47 research-based strategies for the standards-based classroom.* Thousand Oaks, CA: Corwin.

Webb, D., & Webb, T. (1990). *Accelerated learning with music.* Norcross, GA: Accelerated Learning Systems.

Westwater, A., & Wolfe, P. (2000). The brain-compatible curriculum. *Educational Leadership, 58*(3), 49–52.

Wiggins, G., & McTighe, J. (2008). Put understanding first. *Educational Leadership, 65*(19), 36–41.

Willis, J. (2007, summer). *The neuroscience of joyful education.* Retrieved July 20, 2007, from www.ascd.org.80.

Wolfe, P. (2001). *Brain matters: Translating research into classroom practice.* Alexandria, VA: Association for Supervision and Curriculum Development.

Wolfe, P., & Nevills, P. (2004). *Building the reading brain. PreK–3.* Thousand Oaks, CA: Corwin.

Wonacott, M. E. (1993). *Apprenticeship and the future of the workplace.* Retrieved September 3, 2009, from http://www.ericdigests.org/1992–3/future.htm.

Index